Handbook on Mushrooms

Fourth Edition

Dr (Mrs) Nita Bahl

Oxford & IBH Publishing Co. Pvt. Ltd.
New Delhi
(A Unit of CBS Publishers & Distributors Pvt Ltd)

CBS Publishers & Distributors Pvt Ltd

New Delhi • Bengaluru • Chennai • Kochi • Kolkata • Lucknow • Mumbai
Hyderabad • Jharkhand • Nagpur • Patna • Pune • Uttarakhand

Handbook on Mushrooms Fourth Edition

ISBN-13: 978-81-204-1399-3
ISBN-10: 81-204-1399-7

Reprint: 2015, 2018, **2024**

OXFORD & IBH
New Delhi
(*A Unit of* CBS Publishers & Distributors Pvt Ltd)

Published by **Satish Kumar Jain** and produced by **Varun Jain** for

CBS Publishers & Distributors Pvt Ltd

4819/XI Prahlad Street, 24 Ansari Road, Daryaganj, New Delhi 110 002, India.
Ph: 011-23289259, 23266838 Website: www.cbspd.com
e-mail: delhi@cbspd.com

Corporate Office: 204 FIE, Industrial Area, Patparganj, Delhi 110 092
Ph: 011-4934 4934 Fax: 011-4934 4935
e-mail: publishing@cbspd.com; publicity@cbspd.com

Branches

- **Bengaluru:** Seema House 2975, 17th Cross, KR Road, Banasankari 2nd Stage, Bengaluru 560 070, Karnataka, India
  Ph: +91-80-26771678/79 Fax: +91-80-26771680 e-mail: bangalore@cbspd.com
- **Chennai:** 7, Subbaraya Street, Shenoy Nagar, Chennai 600 030, Tamil Nadu, India
  Ph: +91-44-26680620, 26681266 Fax: +91-44-42032115 e-mail: chennai@cbspd.com
- **Kochi:** 42/1325, 1326, Power House Road, Opp KSEB, Power House, Ernakulum Kochi 682 018, Kerala, India
  Ph: +91-484-4059061-65,67 Fax: +91-484-4059065 e-mail: kochi@cbspd.com
- **Kolkata:** 147, Hind Ceramics Compound, 1st Floor, Nilgunj Road, Belghoria, Kolkata-700056, West Bengal, India
  Ph: +033-25633055, 033-25633056 e-mail: kolkata@cbspd.com
- **Lucknow:** Basement, Khushnuma Complex, 7 Meerabai Marg (Behind Jawahar Bhawan), Lucknow-226001, UP, India
  Ph: +0522-4000032 e-mail: tiwari.lucknow@cbspd.com
- **Mumbai:** PWD Shed, Gala no 25/26, Ramchandra Bhatt Marg, Next to JJ Hospital Gate no. 2, Opp. Union Bank of India, Noorbaug, Mumbai-400009, Maharashtra, India
  Ph: 022-66661880/89 e-mail: mumbai@cbspd.com

Representatives

- Hyderabad 0-9885175004
- Patna 0-9334159340
- Jharkhand 0-9811541605
- Pune 0-9664372571
- Nagpur 0-8692091830
- Uttarakhand 0-9716462459

Printed at Chaman Enterprises, Daryaganj, Delhi, India

Preface to the Fourth Edition

India is fast emerging as a major mushroom producing country during last 5 years there is perceptible change in scenario, particularly in respect of production system, horizontal spread and vertical growth in productivity. Recent advancement have laid to almost five times increase in total production of mushroom in the country. The rate of increase in production is about 35–40% as against the global growth rate of about 7%. It is obvious to sustain this kind of growth rate, cultivation should be done under controlled conditions. Recent advances in cultivation of button mushroom around the year, made it very essential to up date the book giving farm layout, land requirement and economics involved in it, as well as other important cultivable mushroom.

Nita Bahl

Preface to the First Edition

Increase in population is creating an alarming situation in the food problem in India. Malnutrition in terms of 'protein' deficiency is becoming a major hazard in developing countries.

Exploiting non-traditional food resources can make a substantial breakthrough to meet the serious food deficit. In this circumstance, popularising mushroom as part and parcel of every day food is of paramount importance.

No food is so wrapped in mystery as mushroom. It is amazing to see tiny pin heads on a tray of dung and straw growing into buttons rich in protein, vitamins and minerals. However, it is unfortunate to realise that mushrooms did not receive universal acceptance over the years, since a number of naturally growing mushrooms are poisonous. Today the situation has changed because the cultivated edible species of mushrooms are totally safe for human consumption.

Mushroom farming is becoming successful because of its very low inputs. It is estimated that about 300 million tonnes of fresh mushroom can be produced for just one-fourth of world's annual yield of straw (2,325 million tonnes). Such an amount would provide 4,100 million people with 250 g of fresh mushroom daily.

In India, mushroom growing can be highly rewarding because of a variable climate. The technology can be profitably considered in areas where land is a limiting factor and agricultural residues are abundantly available. The cultivation of three types of mushrooms, white button (*Agaricus bisporus*), paddy straw (*Volvariella* spp.) and Dhingri (*Pleurotus* spp.), which can be grown at different temperatures in different seasons, have been intensified, thus, making mushroom a year-round crop.

Literature on cultivation under Indian conditions are scattered and are available only in the form of pamphlets. Therefore, it is anticipated that this 'Handbook on Mushrooms' will serve as an indispensable guide not only to mushroom growers, research workers and teachers but also to enthusiastic housewives.

I am highly indebted to Drs. (Miss) Shashi Prabba Lal and (Mrs.) Padma Ramachandran for their ungrudging help in critically going through the manuscript and proof reading. Thanks are due to Dr. P.N. Chowdhari for rendering his help from time to time.

Thanks are also due to my family for their co-operation to fulfil the assignment.

Nita Bahl

Foreword

The use of mushrooms as human food dates back to antiquity. In ancient cultures such as the Indian, Greek, and Roman, mushrooms have been described as sophisticated delicacies associated with Royal class. And today with the development of better technologies and greater realization of their nutrient values, mushrooms have come to occupy an important place in food habits of people in several parts of the world.

Commercial cultivation of mushrooms started in Europe at the turn of last century. With increasing scientific research in the biology of mushrooms and more improvised techniques for growing them, mushroom cultivation has almost become an industry in several countries like U.S.A., U.K., France and the Netherlands.

With all their historical background and nutritive importance, it is unfortunate that in India mushrooms have not caught the imagination of the public at large to become an important food item. This is particularly paradoxical, since it could become an important source of nutritive proteins and minerals to the vast number of vegetarians. Perhaps the reasons for their not being taken up widely is their non-availability at low prices for the common man and also due to lack of knowledge of their cultivation methods. Hence, it is necessary that a large number of people are made aware of the simple methods required for successful cultivation of edible mushrooms.

Keeping this in view, I consider the *Handbook on Mushrooms* by Mrs. Nita Bahl is very timely. Besides enumerating the various aspects of mushroom morphology, food value, etc., the author has elaborately described the pros and cons of mushrooms cultivation, particularly of the edible white button (*Agaricus bisporus*), paddy straw (*Volvariella* spp.) and Dhingri (*Pleurotus* spp.). The data on economics, I guess, should provide an impetus to any reader to start home growing of edible mushrooms. I sincerely hope that this book will greatly benefit all those involved in scientific research and training on mushrooms as also those venturing to make mushroom growing a useful and an enterprising profession.

Deputy Director General (CS) M.V. Rao
Indian Council of Agricultural Research
Krishi Bhavan, New Delhi

Contents

Chapter 1

Introduction

Fungi have been at work since life began on earth. To quote Carlyle "Nature alone is antique and the oldest art a mushroom."

There are different views in regard to the origin of the term "mushroom". In Latin, 'fungo" means to flourish. It was a term which was used to refer to mushroom and to excrescences from the ground or from trees. In Greek the term "mushroom", was derived from the word "sphonggos" or "sphoggos" which meant "sponge" and referred to the sponge-like structure of some of the species. The word mushroom is usually thought to be derived from the French "mcusseron" (muceron), "mousse" or "moss", but it is not used in quite the same sense. It has been said that "mousseron" is a barbarous name which has caused endless confusion. Other versions are "muscheron" and "mouscheron" and from these it is easy to understand how the country name of "mushroom" originated.

Three and half millenia ago, the Greek hero Perseus, in fulfilment of the pronouncement of an oracle, accidentally killed his grandfather Acrisius whom he was to succeed on the throne of Agros. According to Parasanians, when Perseus returned to Agros, ashamed of his deed, he persuaded Megapenthes, son of Proteus, to exchange their kingdoms. When he had received the kingdom of Proteus he founded Mycenae, because his cap (mykes) had fallen off and he regarded this as a sign to found a city. It is also believed that, being thirsty, he chanced to take up a mushroom (mykes) and drank the water flowing from it. Pleased, he gave the place the name of Mycenae. Thus one of the greatest civilisations of history, Mycenae, may have been named after a legendary mushroom. Mycenae is derived from the same Greek word mycology (mykes—mushroom + logos—discourse, Alexopoulos, 1962).

The earliest word in Sanskrit for mushroom appears to be *ksumpa*. In present day Hindi, it is evolved into *khumbi*. The word *chatra* is a later one which is given to the fleshy-capped fungi. Other words are *kukurmutta, kavaka, bhoomi kavak* and *bhustrna*.

The invasion (migration) of the Aryans into the Indian subcontinent took place around 1500 B.C. They carried with them an intoxicating drink *soma*. *Soma* was mostly used in Aryan religious rites. In the *Rig Veda* there are many songs on *soma*. According to Wasson (1969) the *soma* in the *Rig Veda* refers to *Amanita muscaria*.

The cult based on devotion to fungi is not unique to any country or to any time. Mushrooms have been worshipped since long and in some primitive cultures are still considered divine.

Historical records about the beginning of human culture are insufficient and the indications of prehistoric people using fungi are very rare. O'Heer (1886) and others have found traces of puffballs and other fungi carved on stones. In Central America and the highlands of Guatemala mushroom-shaped stone carvings have also been found. These are considered to belong to the Mayan period and point to the fact that these were used in ceremonies, etc. Mayancodices which contain religious and astrological paintings depict figures offering or holding mushroom shaped objects. These objects resemble very closely the fruit body of *Amanita muscaria* (the fly agaric). It is only from classical times that various names for fungi have been given such as *Bolites, Agarikon, Amanita*, etc.

Mushrooms appeal to different people in different ways. They are objects of beauty for artists, and for medical people they are the possible source of new drugs. Architects have constructed minarets, temples and cupola columns in its shape. Jewellers have made expensive pieces on mushroom designs. Designers have reproduced the mushroom design on fabrics. Bulgaria has issued a series of nine stamps on mushrooms. The most luxurious feasts in Roman times used to be of those in which mushroom preparations were served. In one of his satires the Roman poet Horace (born 65 B.C.) praises "Pratanses", presumably field mushroom, as the best of fungi. The Roman naturalist Pliny who died in A.D. 79 described *Amanita caesaria* and *Boletus edulis* as delicacies and also spoke of mushroom preparations which were served in special and costly utensils only to masters. The Romans were as sophisticated in their eating habits as they were in the fine arts.

The use of mushroom as food goes back to the farthest antiquity. They have been gathered on a considerable scale throughout the world. Aristocrats offered high prices for these and they were delicacies for princes. In the Continent a special code of law was also made to deal with the search for truffles and dogs, pigs and bears were trained for this purpose.

There are many fairy tales and folk songs about mushrooms. The ancient Indian, Greek and Roman myths agree that mushrooms sprang from a stroke of lightning. In Mexico, Indians believed that mushrooms are sacred because they are born of the sexual intercourse between a bolt of lightning and the earth. There are lots of superstitions about the mushroom. Regarding fairy rings, it was once believed that fairies used to dance at midnight in circles but actually the dark green circles in the grass around which mushrooms appear are caused by the radial growth of the fungus in the soil. Another delightful superstition is mentioned in "Alice in Wonderland", when a bite of one side of a certain mushroom would make one grow and a bite of the other side would make one smaller, so by a little judicious nibbling it was possible to adjust oneself to any dimension.

Some mushrooms are edible while others are poisonous. Poisonous mushrooms are known as toad-stools though this is not a scientific term. In olden days, before people could differentiate between edible and non-edible mushrooms, many lives were perhaps lost by the consumption of non-edible mushrooms. Classical writings give many references in which the harmful effects of mushrooms were noted before their use as food was recorded. There is no general rule for the identification of poisonous and non-poisonous mushrooms. There are many traditional methods for testing these fungi but they are unreliable. It was believed that mushrooms which grew in the meadows were edible and those which grew among rusty nails, rotten eggs, near serpent holes or on trees producing poisonous fruits were not edible.

The belief was prevalent that edible mushroom peeled off easily and did not change a silver spoon black while cooking. This belief is incorrect as *Amanita phalloides*, which is poisonous, peels off easily and the silver spoon remains unaffected. It was also held that brightly coloured mushrooms were poisonous whereas white or creamy ones were edible. This is also wrong as "Chanterelle" (*Cantharellus cibarius*) and "Wood Blewits" (*Tricholoma nuduns*), even though bright coloured, are quite safe to eat whereas the "Death cap" (*Amanita phalloides*), "Fool's mushroom" (*Amanita verna*) and "Destroying angel" (*Amanita verosa*) are completely white and deadly poisonous.

Feeding doubtful specimens to dogs or cats is also useless as the reactions may be different or slower in these cases. It is not safe to believe that fungi which have been nibbled by slugs or larvae are not poisonous; on the contrary, slugs seem to be particularly fond of *Amanita phalloides* and the stomach contents of rabbits are able to neutralise the poison of the most dangerous species. Some refer to colour and shape, smell and taste, exudation of milk when broken or change in colour of flesh, coagulation of milk, etc. as pointers to the edibility or otherwise, of a mushroom but these are all incorrect. To give an example, the yellow staining mushroom *Agaricus xanthoderma* quickly changes from white to yellow where it is touched or rubbed and later from yellow changes to chocolate. Similarly, *Boletus satanas* changes to bluish-green when it is damaged, but both are poisonous.

It was also thought that one genus, mostly having the edible species, would not include the poisonous ones but this is also a wrong notion. Some species of one particular genus may be edible whereas the other may be highly poisonous. The genus *Agaricus*, for instance, includes on the one hand, the common edible species, *A. arvensis* and *A. campestris* and, on the other hand, also includes poisonous species like *A. xanthoderma.* A genus having many poisonous species may also have non-poisonous species. *Amanita*, for instance, includes the highly poisonous species *A. phalloides*, *A. verna*, and *A. verosa* and it also includes the edible species *A. rubescense.*

Two mushrooms may possess a morphologically close resemblance but one may be edible and the other may be non-edible. Only by knowing the distinguishing characters one can separate the two. *Lepiota margani,* for instance, is a poisonous mushroom and if eaten causes a fatal illness whereas *Lepiota rachodes* is edible and delicious. These two species are so closely related to each other and look so greatly alike that only an expert can separate and distinguish them, by the fact that mature specimens of *L. margani* (poisonous) have green gills and pale green spore deposits whereas the spores and gills of *L. rachodes* are white. Half-grown specimens of both kinds are identical. People who know those mushrooms claim that a specimen found in autumn is edible but not the one found in spring. This contention is usually correct but sometimes both species come up together in autumn and people who depend upon the season of appearance, instead of spore colour to distinguish them may suffer seriously for their careless collection and eating.

In every country wild mushrooms are sold. *Gyromitra esculenta,* the common brown "Saddle fungus" was considered to be of good taste and was sold in the big markets of Europe and America. After some time, however, its sale was banned in those countries because it was proved beyond doubt to be deadly poisonous and had taken many lives. Some believe that there are two varieties of

Gyromitra esculenta, one being edible and the other non-edible, others believe that all individuals of this species contain a toxin which is water soluble; leaches out in the water in which the mushrooms are cooked and that if this water is poured off, the mushrooms are good to eat. Still others believe that this fungus is poisonous only when eaten by sick or undernourished people, especially children or if eaten in excessive quantities. It is true that under certain circumstances it causes illness.

It is possible that certain geographical races of mushrooms may be poisonous while others may not be so. Possibly a species may be edible when it is young and fresh and may become poisonous when it is overmatured and has started decaying. On the other hand, the method of preparation may destroy the poisonous substance that is present in uncooked mushroom. It is also believed that the mushroom will lose its toxicity if it is maintained for several days in water and vinegar, but this is not true. Such treatment may eliminate the bitter taste and irritants from the mushroom but it does not remove the poison of the dangerous species. In reports, that a certain mushroom is edible at times while at other times it proves to be poisonous, may be attributed to any one of these reasons.

It must be remembered that even edible mushrooms can cause indigestion in healthy people and some people may be allergic to a species which is harmless to others. Causes of discomfort and indigestion may be due to eating too much, or eating mushrooms with indigestible food, or the fungi being past maturity or having been incorrectly cooked. Mushrooms may also cause illness if alcohol is taken at the same meal. For instance, purplish red skin discolouration may occur as a temporary result of eating the "Ink cap" (*Coprinus atramentarius*) variety with alcohol.

Eating poisonous mushrooms may result in different types of reactions which can be classified as follows:

Nervous Disorder

The poison causes degeneration of cells of the organisms particularly of the nervous system and glandular parenchymatous tissues (liver etc.). This happens in the case of poisoning by *Amanita phalloides.*

Gastric Disorder

(a) The poison causes serious gastric disturbances, acts chiefly by exciting and then paralysing the central nervous system e.g., *Amanita muscaria.* (b) Poison-containing irritant which cause gastrocenteritis by direct action on the mucous membrane of the digestive system e.g., *Gyromitra esculenta.*

Haemolytic Disorder

Mushrooms like *Amanita rubescens* contain haemolytic or blood-destroying principles.

Muscular Disorder

Mushrooms having substance which excite the muscular system especially the smooth muscle fibres (the uterus, vessels, etc.)

If anybody has the ill-effect of mushroom poisoning, the severity of an attack and its after effects can be considerably lessened by prompt treatment, so it is desirable that everyone who is in the habit of collecting and eating these fungi, shoud be capable of applying first-aid remedies.

When anyone, after eating mushroom develops symptoms described above, no time should be lost in summoning a doctor, who should be informed of the nature of the case which he is required to attend so that he should bring necessary appliances. In the mean time, preliminary treatment may be given. The general aims of the treatment are :

1) to remove from the system the remains of the fungi eaten,

2) to bring about the elimination or exhaustion of the toxins already absorbed by the blood,

3) to counteract pain and all other distressing symptoms, and

4) to guard against collapse and generally to keep a watch on the action of the heart.

Treatment

1) *Expulsion of the fungus.* In cases of poisoning, the usual procedure is to try immediately to endure vomiting. In some cases, however, if the patient is unable to vomit, then a tablespoonful of mustard in half a glass of warm water should be given. Apomorphine, tartar emetic or zinc sulphate may alternatively be used. Since, however, each is in itself a powerful poison, any of these should only be employed under medical direction. On no account should salt and water be administered, as unless this acts at once, it merely accentuates the solubility of the poisons.

If possible, the stomach should afterwards be washed out by means of stomach tube or failing this, copious draughts of warm water should be given.

After this treatment, the next step is to administer a purgative, preferably of an alkaline nature, such as one to two level desert spoonful of either sulphate of soda (glauber's salt) or sulphate of magnesium (Epsom salt) in a glass of warm water. If there is griping pain in the stomach the above should be substituted for one tablespoonful of castor oil in a little milk. Another soothing drink is two tablespoonful of olive oil, beaten up with the yolk of an egg and four or five tablespoonful of milk or warm water, to which, under the doctor's instructions, twenty drops of landanum may be added.

2) *Elimination of the toxin.* The natural elimination or exhaustion of the poison which has already been absorbed into the blood, can only be expedited or assisted by subcutaneous injections of atropine; or other medical means.

3) The counteraction of the various distressing symptoms which almost always accompany an attack of fungus poisoning should likewise be left in the hands of the doctor. In case of delirium, sedatives such as potassium bromide are necessary. Lethargy and depression can be treated by strong tea, coffee, etc. Pain can be treated by the use of opium compounds, while prolonged and excessive vomiting can be checked with soda water (aerated water) or by giving the patient small pieces of ice to suck.

4) *Effect on the heart.* Many mushrooms have a marked effect on the heart's action, so stimulants can be given.

Chapter 2

History of Mushroom Cultivation

Mushrooms have been considered a delicacy for several thousand years. In the ancient Greek and Roman literature we find references to mushrooms. The first record of the cultivation of mushrooms was during the reign of Louis XIV (1638–1715). The earliest description and knowhow of growing mushrooms was written by de Tourneforte, a Frenchman, and it was published in Paris in 1707. The method described by him is remarkably similar to that employed today. In fact, no radical changes took place until as recently as 75 years ago.

In 1800, the French started growing mushrooms underground in the quarries around Paris, on horse manure which was stacked in heaps and allowed to heat up naturally. The resulting compost was laid down in long ridges and inoculated with spawn dug from meadows or mill tracts where horses had been trampling. It was just a matter of chance if one got a mushroom crop from that compost. Treschow pointed out that shortly before 1700 it was a fashion to grow melon and pineapple in hot beds under heat; spontaneous and frequent appearance of *A. bisporus* in the composted manure in the hot beds was observed several times. This suggested a method of growing *A. bisporus.* Besides perfection of the French mushroom-growing methods and its quantitative development which took place early, mushroom production remained rather stationary till recent years. Finally, refined methods were introduced as a result of the investigations of the French mycologists. Thus in France, mushrooms were produced in large quantities in catacombs, caves and quarries around Paris, with a composting procedure essentially comparable with the one used today. English growers were quick to take advantage of the extensive and natural supplies of wild spawn in the country and 80 years ago they were exporting spawn to America, Germany, Denmark and Australia. By the end of the nineteenth century, French mycologists, among them Matrochot and Costantin (1894), succeeded in solving two important problems in mushroom cultivation. First, they discovered the cause of the mushroom disease, *la mole* (*Mycogone perniciosa* Magnus) and started fumigating with sulphur; and secondly, they were able to germinate spores for the purpose of obtaining sterile spawn. This was probably the most important contribution to scientifically controlled mushroom growing. The process was patented but did not appear to have been commercialised, and in 1902 Miss Fergussen of Corne described in detail methods for germinating spores. Duggar (1905) perfected in America, method of making pure culture spawn from mushroom tissue. This method was exploited immediately, the Americans realised that now it was possible to select and guarantee a particular strain. From that moment mushroom growing began to develop into highly scientific industry, that it is today.

In 1918, the U.S. marketed pure spore culture bottled spawn introduced by Lambert. It was produced by spores from mushroom (selected for its size, colour and appearance), germinating them under aseptic conditions and then injecting into a bottle of sterilised horse manure compost. The culture was prepared in ordinary milk bottles and the contents were protected during the growing period by means of cotton wool plugs. When the compost was permeated with mycelium, the bottle was broken and the spawn was ready for planting. Other conditions being perfect, the grower was assured of a crop. Many European countries started the production of pure-culture spawn (circa, 1918). At any rate, the availability of plenty of sterile and uniform spawn issued by trustworthy private and government laboratories had given the starting signal to the mass production of mushrooms.

It has been suggested that cultivation above ground originated in Sweden. Lundberg described mushroom growing in greenhouses in 1754. Callow (1831) reports that a house of a peculiar construction, after the German practice, was introduced by Oldacre (gardener to the late Sir Joseph Banks). The house was warmed by fire heat and recommended as one well adapted to the growth of mushroom throughout the year. Callow described and sketched one such house in England in which he grew mushrooms on a flat bed on the ground (instead of the customary ridge bed) and on shelves one above the other on brackets attached to the walls. This is the earliest record known in which shelf beds are mentioned.

It was only during the last 50 years, however, that a standard American mushroom house was evolved to bring the growers within reach of controlled temperature, humidity and aeration all the year round. With well-insulated walls and a false ceiling, it was possible for growers to manipulate ventilation and the heating system. Besides, the small shelves bracketed to the walls were replaced by half a dozen or more wide shelves on an independent wooden framework. Although in the later years of the last century French growers had discovered that ground gypsum (calcium sulphate) prevented greasiness in the compost. Pizer, at Wye College in 1936, discovered that gypsum immensively improve spawn growth in compost which is now universally accepted. Concurrently, much study was in progess concerning diseases and competitive moulds mainly by Ware, Glassoock and Bewley in U.K. and by Lambert and Beach in America. Bewley and Lambert also did useful preliminary work on the relationship between compost and yield. Growers started to realise that a good compost was almost as important as a good soil. Lambert and Sinden were working on synthetic composts. Sinden patented his grain spawn process in 1932. Pests remained a serious menace, despite the invaluable investigation of Thomas, Austin and Jary.

During the Second World War, the Ministry of Agriculture declared that mushrooms not only possessed high food value but competed with more favoured vegetables for the limited supply of fertilisers (mainly horse manure which was becoming alarmingly scarce). In consequence, mushroom was the one vegetable specifically prohibited as a crop under glass and elsewhere its growth was discouraged by withdrawal of labour. In 1945, a number of specialists calling themselves the Midlands Group of Mushroom Growers held a series of meetings to discuss the problem facing the industry resulting before long in the formation of associations like M.G.A. (Mushroom Growers' Association of England and Ireland) as a specialist branch of the National Farmers' Union; the M.R.A. (Mushroom Research Association Ltd.) was launched to investigate the cultural problems; and the M.G.P. (Midlands Group of Publication) was established to commission authoritative leaflets on the technical aspects of commercial growing and to publish the M.G.A. bulletin.

The M.G.A., during its first five years of existence, secured government recognition of the fact of the mushroom being a food of value. Essential materials such as fuel, gypsum and timber were made available when supplies became difficult. Advice on a multitude of questions is available to *bonafide* growers on an increasingly helpful scale.

The M.R.S. (Mushroom Research Station) at Yaxley produced during its short life, a formula for synthetic compost which could replace manure commercially and also made useful recommendations on a number of problems such as the control of truffle disease and during preliminary work on casings proved the usefulness of peat which is now very widely used.

In the scientific field, research is developing fast in Europe and America. At the G.C.R.I. at Littlehampton, much work is being done on the control of cecids, phorids and mites, virus and bacterial diseases, compost, casing and environment, genetics, nutrition and nematode control.

In Denmark, Rasmussen produced startling results with pig manure and a new experimental plant has been opened at Copenhagen. A fine centre was opened at Horst in Holland in 1959. Arnold in East Germany, Bukowskii in Poland, Hetlay in Hungary and Willianis in Belgium are pushing forward state-sponsored programmes.

Lambert of the U.S.D.A. had laid down the formation of modern mushroom growing whereas Sinden and Tschierpe have done useful work on composting and environmental control. Bels has done much for the benefit of the Dutch mushroom industry. During the past 20 years much headway has been made in the field of mechanisation, i.e., manure turners, spawning, filling and casing of trays by mechanised means. Now attempts are in full swing for the mechanical harvesting of mushroom and the growing of mushrooms in polythene bags. The use of benlate has also enabled production to rise quite dramatically almost everywhere. Japan, Korea, Italy and Malaya are making tremendous contributions in the production of mushrooms in the world.

Present status of the mushroom industry in India

In India, cultivation of edible mushrooms did not exist till recently though methods of cultivation for some have been known for many years. In 1886, some fine specimens of mushrooms were grown by N.W. Newton and exhibited at the annual show of the Horticultural Society of India. In 1908, a thorough search was instituted by Sir David Prain regarding edible mushrooms in India because it attracted his attention as food used by the poor in famine, stricken areas. Bose (1921) was successful in culturing two agarics on a sterilised dung medium, details of which were published in the Indian Science Congress held at Nagpur during 1926. He further suggested its cultivation as a means for raising food for daily consumption and emphasised the importance of the same becoming a major industry in India. The method of growing mushrooms on horse manure was discussed in detail by Bose and Bose (1940). Later on, Padwick (1941) stated that the cultivation of *Agaricus bisporus* was tried all over the world with great success but it often remained unsuccessful in India and pointed out possibilities and obstacles in its cultivation in this country.

Experiments in cultivating the paddy straw mushroom (*Volvariella*) were first undertaken in India by the Agriculture Department, Madras, during 1939 and 1945, although the work was discontinued later. Su and Seth (1940) outlined the procedure of the spawn production of *Volvariella volvacea*. Thomas *et al.* (1943), gave full directions about the cultivation of paddy straw mushroom *(V. diplasia)* in Madras. Asthana (1947) got better yield of paddy straw mushroom by adding powdered red gram dal to the beds. He advocated April to June as being the best period for the cultivation of this mushroom in then Central Provinces and also gave an account of the chemical analysis of the mushroom. A serious attempt was made by the Department of Agriculture. H.P., in collaboration with the ICAR during the year 1961 as a result of which a scheme entitled "Development of Mushroom Cultivation in H.P." was started. Initially, an attempt was made to grow mushrooms on cowdung but this met with partial failure. During 1964, the department succeeded in growing its first mushroom on a horse manure compost and since then the basis for research work has really been established. Similarly, growing mushrooms on a purely synthetic compost using wheat straw and inorganic fertilisers and organic substrates was successfully chosen as an ideal synthetic medium for growing commercial mushroom. Later, results revealed a break-through in the selection of spent compost as a casing soil, in the control of diseases and insect pests with fungicides and insecticides available within the country and the industry began to acquire a strong foothold in these fields.

Commercial mushroom growing was first initiated in New Delhi and Solan and later it spread to Jammu & Kashmir, the Nilgiris, Punjab, Haryana, Chandigarh, Uttar Pradesh, Maharashtra, Madhya Pradesh and Gujarat.

The Indian Council of Agricultural Research (ICAR) sanctioned the creation of National Centre for Mushroom Research and Training (NCMRT) during VIth Plan in October 1982 with the objectives of conducting research on problems of mushroom production, preservation, utilization and to impart training to scientists, teachers, extension workers and interested growers. It also sanctioned an All India Co-ordinated Mushroom Improvement Project (AICMIP) at six centres in five states for multilocational testing of available technology. The centre started functioning at Solan from June 1983.

Chapter 3

Food Value of Mushrooms

Sufficient food supply is a country's most precious asset. With increasing population and conventional agricultural methods we cannot cope with the food problem. In view of the current energy food crisis it has become most important to make a substantial breakthrough in the technology of food production to meet a serious food deficit situation.

A sufficient calorie intake does not guarantee a good standard of nutrition. Food containing minerals, vitamins and enough of the right kind of protein is necessary in addition to that furnishing energy. Protein deficiency is not only a future problem but also an existing reality. Though the protein is synthesised tremendously by green plants, the concentration of protein in plants with a few exceptions is quite low in terms of the percentage of total weight.

Mushrooms provide a rich addition to the diet in the form of protein, carbohydrate, valuable salts and vitamins. As food, the nutritional value of mushroom lies between meat and vegetables. Investigations by Lintzel (1941, 1943) indicate that 100 to 200 g of mushrooms (dry weight) are required to maintain nutritional balance in normal human being weighing 70 kg. They equated the nutritive value of mushrooms to that of muscle protein. Experiments proved that mushrooms are well suited to supplement diets which lack protein and in the sense they have rightly been called "vegetable meat" (Table 3.1).

From the table it is evident that mushrooms provide a high protein and low caloric diet. In other words, they are the number one diet to be recommended to heart patients.

Zakia (1976) has attempted an analysis of edible mushroom (Table 3.2).

A vast literature is available, particularly on the protein content of mushroom. Work on different aspects of mushroom composition is summarised as follows:

Table 3.1. Composition of Cultivated Mushrooms and some Common Vegetables per 100 g of Article (Wooster, 1954)

Name	Calories	Moisture	Fat	Carbo-hydrate %	Protein % (Dry wt. basis)
Beet root	42	87.6	0.1	9.6	12.9
Brinjal	24	92.7	0.2	5.5	15.1
Cabbage	24	92.4	0.2	5.3	18.4
Cauliflower	25	91.7	0.2	4.9	28.8
Celery	18	93.4	0.2	7.7	21.6
Green beans	98	74.3	0.4	17.7	26.1
Lima beans	128	66.5	0.8	23.5	22.2
Mushroom	16	91.1	0.3	4.4	26.9
Potato	83	73.8	0.1	19.1	7.6

Table 3.2. Approximate Analysis of Edible Mushrooms Fresh Weight Basis per cent (Zakia, 1976)

Mushrooms	Moisture	Ash	Protein	Fat	Crude fibre
Agaricus bisporus	89.5	1.25	3.94	0.19	1.09
Lepiota sp.	91.0	1.09	3.3	0.18	0.86
Pleurotus sp.	90.0	0.97	2.78	0.65	1.08
Pleurotus ostreatus	92.5	–	2.15	–	–
Termitomyces sp.	91.3	0.81	4.1	0.22	1.13
Volvariella diplasia	90.4	1.10	3.90	0.25	1.57
Volvariella volvacea	88.4	1.46	4.98	0.74	1.38

Protein

It is possible to grow several heavy crops of mushroom in a year and its intensive cultivation and high yield can compensate for the protein. Hence mushroom can be compared more favourably with other crops in terms of yield per unit area. Cereals, for instance, give an annual yield 3000 to 6000 kg/hectare but mushrooms may give up to 2 million kg/ha (Cooke, 1977). The produce of an acre of land can be transformed into ten times as much fungus protein as meat protein.

The following data show yields of dry protein per unit area utilised for farming beef, fish and *A. bisporus* (Cooke, 1977).

Approximate annual yield dry protein (kg/ha)	
Beef, cattle conventional agriculture	78
Fish-intensive pond rearing	675
Agaricus bisporus	65,000

On an area basis they are a more valuable source of protein than either cattle or fish.

Mushroom contain protein which consists of various amino acids (Table 3.3). All the essential amino acids required by an adult are present in mushrooms (Hayes and Haddad, 1976). Tryptophan and lysine are present in high concentration as compared to cystein and methionine. These amino acids are compared to cystein and methionine. These amino acids are absent in vegetable proteins. Mushroom protein, like other fungal protein, is intermediate in quality between vegetable and animal protein. The supplementary value of mushroom protein in vegetarian diet is, therefore, of considerable significance. Lintzel (1941) reported the digestibility of mushroom protein to be as high as 72 to 83 per cent.

Table 3.3. Amino Acid Composition of *A. Bisporus* (Hayes and Haddad, 1976)

	per 100 g dry matter
Alanine	2.40
Arginine	1.90
Aspartic acid	3.14
Cystine	0.18
Glutamic acid	7.06
Glycine	1.20
Histidine	0.64
Isoleucine	1.28
Leucine	2.16
Lysine	1.62
Methionine	0.39
Phenylalanine	1.55
Proline	2.50
Serine	1.89
Threoenine	1.48
Tryptophan	3.94
Tyrosine	0.78
Valine	1.63

Vitamins

According to Anderson and Fellers (1942), *A. bisporus* does not contain vitamin A, D or E. They found 8.6 mg ascorbic acid, 5.82 mg nicotinic and 2.38 mg pantothenic acid, 0.12 mg thiamin, 0.52 mg riboflavin and 0.018 mg biotin per 1000 g fresh weight. Mushroom is reported to be an excellent source of riboflavin and nicotinic acid (niacin) and a good source of pantothenic acid. It also contains appreciable amounts of thiamin, folic acid and ascorbic acid (Kezeli and Dzabaridze, 1944).

Table 3.4. Vitamin Content of Some of the Edible Mushrooms*

Species	Thiamin	Ribo-flavin	Niacin	Ascorbic acid
Agaricus bisporus	1.1	5.0	55.7	81.9
Lentinus edodes	7.8	4.9	54.9	0.0
Pleurotus ostreatus	4.8	4.7	108.7	0.0
Volvariella volvacea	1.2	3.3	91.9	20.2

*Data presented as milligrams of vitamins per 100 g dry weight.

Minerals

Ash analysis given by Anderson and Fellers (1942) shows that *A. bisporus* contains high amounts of potassium, phosphorus, copper and iron but the calcium percentage is quite low.

Carbohydrates and fats

As indicated in Table 3.1, the carbohydrate and fat content of edible mushrooms is quite low. The absence of starch in mushrooms makes it an ideal food for diabetic patients and for persons who wish to shed excess fat from their bodies.

Table 3.5. Mineral Content of Some of the Edible Mushrooms* (Chang and Hayes, 1978)

Mushroom	Ca	P	Fe	Na	K
Agaricus bisporus	23	1429	0.2	ndb	4762
Lentinus edodes	33	1348	15.2	837	3793
Pleurotus ostreatus	98	476	8.5	61	nd
Volvariella volvacea	71	677	17.1	374	3455

*Data presented as milligrams of minerals per 100 g dry weight

McConnell and Esselen (1947) reported that fresh mushrooms contain 0.95 per cent mannitol, 0.28 per cent reducing sugars, 0.59 per cent glycogen, and 0 91 per cent hemicellulose.

Analysis by Hughes (1962) disclosed that mushrooms are rich in linoleic acid which is an essential fatty acid. There is some evidence that the cream varieties contain more fat than the white varieties.

Energy value of mushrooms

Mushrooms are a good source of energy. Hayes and Haddad (1975) also made similar observations and stated that one pound (454 g) of fresh mushrooms provides 120 k calories. This is nearer to the value given by Watt and Merril (1950) and Morgaeidge (1958) than the generally accepted 32 k calories per pound given by McCanna and Widdowson (1969) and in the Manual of Nutrition. Nevertheless, despite these discrepancies mushrooms can be classed in the category of foods which are low in calories. Since ancient times mushrooms have featured as choice dishes on many a regal table. In Italy, Ceaser relished the flavourful meadow mushrooms. The Chinese of the orient added the delicate fungi to scent their sauces and soups.

Hence, among the many novel sources of food, particularly of protein mushrooms apart from being famous for their appetising flavour, offer themselves as potential protein source to bridge the protein gap. The great advantage is that mushrooms have the capacity to convert nutritionally valueless substances into high protein food.

In a country like India where vegetarians dominate, every attempt should be made to popularise a vegetable protein source like mushroom.

Chapter 4

Uses of Mushrooms

The most important use of mushroom is as an article of food and its value as such is beyond the reach of the chemist or physiologist. In addition, mushrooms possess great value as condiments of food accessories. Mushrooms are among the most appetising of table delicacies and add great flavour to food when cooked with them. Besides being an important food article, mushrooms are variously exploited by man. They are, at the same time, also beneficial to the forest. The forestry mushrooms are nature's most active agents in the disposal of the forests' waste material. There are few species of mushrooms which attack the living trees whereas a large number of them grow on fallen timber, bark, sap wood, etc. The mycelium of mushroom grows in a few years and the complete disintegration of the wood takes place. It gradually mixes with forest soil and provides food for the living trees. Thus mushrooms are one of the most important agents in providing available food for the virgin forest. The role of mushrooms in disposing of the fallen timber in forest and converting dead trees and fallen leaves into available food is most important in maintaining an ecological balance in the forests. Mushrooms, then, are to be given a very high rank among the natural agencies which have contributed to the good of the world.

In addition to their fascination for the gourmet, mushrooms are also utilised for making various articles.

The fruit bodies of *Fomes fomentarius* and *Ganoderma applanatum* are still used to produce a suede-like material from which hats, various articles of dress, handbags and picture frames are made. Dried *Coriolus versicolor* brackets have been used for making hats for costume decoration, while bottle corks are made from *Polyporus squamosus*. *Polyporus applanatus* is used as a curio and also for the purpose of etching. Some species of *Polyporus* have been used for making rajor strop. *Polyporus squamosus* and *P. betulinus* are suitable for this purpose.

Daedalea quercina is sometimes used to clean down horses, particularly those whose skin is too tender for an ordinary curry-comb. It is also used by men for cleaning hair.

Tinder mushrooms: Polyporus fomentarius or "tinder mushroom" sometimes called "German tinder" was used in the manufacturing of tinder.

Tunbridgeware: When Green oak is attacked by *Chlorosplenium aeruginosum,* the tissues become stained with green, giving a very pleasing effect. Wood so affected is used in the manufacture of "Tunbridgeware" and fancy work.

Snuff: Polyporus nigricans when dried and pounded, is an ingredient in snuff.

Dyeing: Polyporus bispidus which gives a brown dye is used for colouring silk, cotton and wool. This is used by leather dressers to give a fawn chestnut colour and by carpenters to give a brown colour to furniture. *P. sulphureus* gives a yellow colour and *Fomes ignitarius* gives a brown black colour. Many other mushrooms are also used for giving different colours.

Writing material: Inky cap mushroom *Coprinus comatus* is very deliquecscent and soon becomes black liquid which can be used for writing purposes.

Mushrooms used for flower pots: Shaped fruit bodies of *Polyporus fomentarius* and *P. ignitarius* are used for flower pots. The tube portion is cut out and the hoofed portion is inverted and hanged. This serves as a receptacle for the soil in which plants are grown.

Luminosity: The ability of organism to produce light in the dark is well known in bacteria, plants and animals. Many fungi are also luminescent and either the fruit body or mycelium or both may be luminous, depending on the species. Luminous wood is well known to woodmen, foresters, timber men and others who have occasion to pass through a wood in darkness. The decayed wood itself when permeated with the mycelium of *Armillaria mellea*, glows strongly as long as growth continues and it remains damp. *Fome anosus* is also a luminous fungus. This fungus grows in mines and both the mycelium and fruit bodies are luminous.

Pleurotus japonicus also emits light. Light is emitted from the gills of *P. japonicus.* A single body can give so much luminosity that one can see Roman letters four-tenths of an inch wide. Other spp. are *Boletus edulis, Collybia longipes,* etc. The luminosity is often so bright that when brought near a printed page in the dark, words can be read.

Hallucination: It is said, "the effect of creating hallucination is not to enable you to remember back, but rather to forget and to imagine you are otherwise than what you are." The hallucinogenic mushrooms are *Amanita muscaria*, several spp. of *Stropharia* and *Psilocybe.* In *Amanita muscaria*, the drug-like stimulant is not decomposed in the stomach but apparently is excreted unchanged in the urine. Many writers have commented on the common practice of renewing the stimulation by drinking the urine of someone who has already eaten the mushroom. The hallucinogenic principle in *Psilocybe* is due to the derivatives Psilocybin and Psilocin. The hallucinogenic effect of Psilocybin is similar to that of LSD. (Psilocybin has been used in the treatment of mental disorders.)

Use as medicines : Many fungi today have been used for medicinal purposes. *Polyporus officinalis* was used under the name "agerick." It was taken internally as a sort of universal remedy for all complaints and disorders. *P. officinalis* was used in homes as a drastic purge and applied externally to stop bleeding. It was also used for chronic catarrh diseases of the breast and lungs, as remedy for night sweating in tuberculosis, for rheumatism, gout, jaundice, dropsy and intestinal worms. It is used in homeopathic doses e.g. *Boletus laricis* (*Agaricus albus*) and Jew's ear (*Auricularia auricula*) was frequently used as a poultice for inflamed eyes and as a gargle for inflammation of the throat.

Fomes ignarius and *F. fomentarius* and surgeon agaricks is used for rapid coagulation of blood.

Lycoperdon gigantenum is used as a soft and comfortable surgical dressing.

Clavatia gigantia is still used for anaesthesia.

Amanita muscaria has been used therapeutically from the earliest times as a powder or tincture for swollen glands, epilepsy and various diseases. It is still used today in homeopathic doses under the name of *Agaricus muscarius.* It is used in highly diluted preparations for heart ailment and rheumatoid arthritis. From *Volvariella volvacea* and *Flammulina velutipes* cardiotoxic proteins have been isolated. They lower the blood pressure and are also active against tumour cells. Anticancerous extract of Shiitake causes recession of some kinds of cancer and inhibits the growth of some viruses like influenza (Edwards, 1975).

Chapter 5

Morphology of Mushroom

Mushroom is a general term applied to the fruiting bodies of the fleshy fungi and as such belongs to different groups of fungi. The majority of these mushrooms (fleshy fungi) belong to Hymenomycetes of Basidiomycotina, characterised by the presence of spore bearing layer known as Hymenium. This layer may be present on either side of the gills as in the gill fungi e.g., *Agaricus;* it may form the lining of the numerous pores present in the fruiting body e.g., *Boletus*; it may form the covering layer of teeth-like structures as in *Hydnum*; or it may cover the more or less upright club or branched fructification e.g., *Clavaria.* In the puff balls (*Lycoperdon*) belonging to Gasteromycetes, the basidiospores are produced and matured inside a closed saccate fruiting structure which opens by an apical pore at maturity.

Other fleshy fungi, viz., *Morchella* belong to the Discomycetes (Ascomycotina). Here in contrast to basidiospores, ascospores are produced inside a sac-like ascus and bear generally two to eight ascospores. These asci may be intermixed with paraphyses and form the hymenium, lining the fruiting body, which may be cup-shaped apothecia, e.g., *Aleuria,* others may resemble basidiocarps, which are clavate to pieleate with the surface convoluted, wrinkled or pitted as in *Morchella.* This is also commonly known as "sponge mushroom" or the morels. However, the common term "mushroom" often refers to the fruiting body of the gill fungi. The following parts of the carpophore or the fruiting structure can easily be distinguished (Fig. 5.1).

The cap or pileus

It is the expanded portion of the carpophore which may be thick, fleshy, membranous or corky and varies greatly in shape, size and colour. The surface of the pileus may be smooth, hairy or rough.

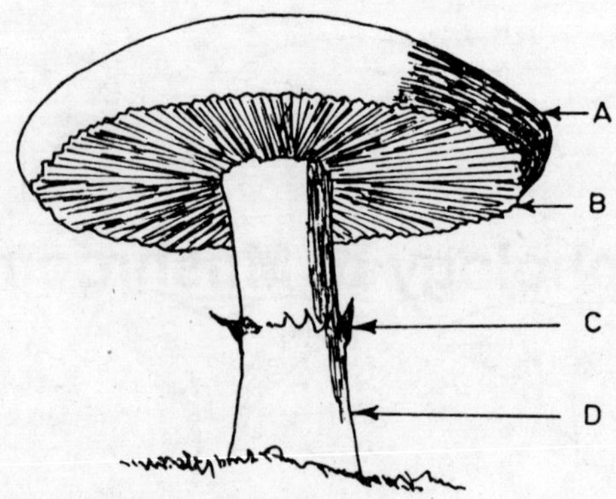

Fig. 5.1 Structure of Mushroom: A—The cap or pileus; B—The gills or lamellae; C—The stalk or stipe.

The gills or lamellae

They are situated on the underside of the pileus starting from the apex of the stalk and radiate out towards the margin. These gills bear spores on their surface and exhibit a change in colour corresponding to that of the spores. For instance, in *Agaricus bisporus* the colour of the young carpophore's gill is pink. With age the colour changes to dark purple, brown or nearly black due to the changing colour of the spores. The attachment of the gill to the stipe helps in the identification of the mushroom (Fig. 5.2). When the gills do not touch the stipe or only do so by a fine line they are known as *Free.* When they are attached directly to the stem, forming nearly a right angle with the latter, they are termed as *Adnate.* If the attachment is only by a part of the width of the gills, they are *Adnexed.* When the gills extend down the stem to a greater or lesser degree they are known as *Decurrent* and when they are near the stalk in a deep notch they are termed as *Sinuate.*

Structure of the gills: An examination of a section through the gills shows the microscopic details (Fig. 5.3). The centre of the gill is made up of mycelial threads known as *Trama;* these threads may run parallel to each other or may be interwoven. Accordingly, the cells may be long or short. Towards the outside of the trama, the cells branch into short cells forming a thin layer, the *Subhymenium.* The subhymenium gives rise to long club-shaped cells which are parallel to each other and at right angles to the surface of the gills. These club-shaped cells are called *Basidia* which have 2 to 4 spine-like projections, the *Sterigmata,* on which *Basidiospores* are borne. Among the *Basidia* there are many sterile cells. Some inflated blad-

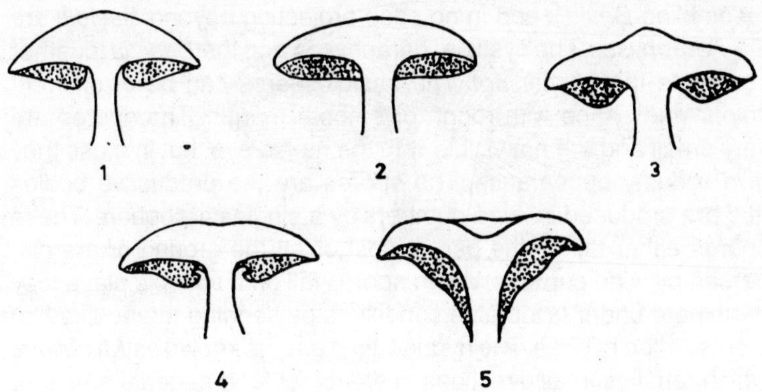

Fig. 5.2 Attachment of gills : (1) Free; (2) Adnate; (3) Adnexed; (4) Sinuate; (5) Decurrent.

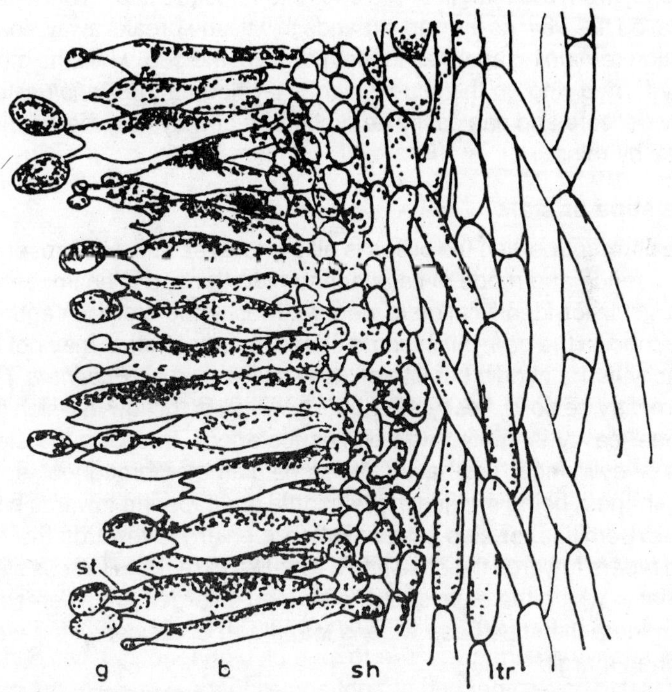

Fig. 5.3 *Agaricus campestris.* Section of gill showing tr = trama; sn = subhymenium; b = basidium the basidia make up the hymenium; st = sterigma; g = spore (magnified).

der like projecting beyond the *Basidia* are the *Cystidia* and those resembling *Basidia* and in no case projecting beyond *Basidia* are the *Paraphyses.* The cystidia, paraphyses and the *Basidia* together constitute the *Hymenium.* The basidiospores can be of different colour and shape with rough or smooth margin. The spores are very small and are not visible with the naked eye, but in mass they give a dusty appearance. The spores are the productive bodies and are produced in large numbers by a single carpophore. These spores either fall on the parent host or on the ground or are dispersed by wind currents. When spores fall on a suitable place they germinate under favourable conditions by sending thread-like filaments called hyphae. The hyphae *en masse* is known as *Mycelium,* which ramifies in all directions in search of food material and after sometime forms fructification under suitable conditions.

The veil

In young fruiting bodies the gill remain covered by a tissue that extends from the margin of the cap (pileus) to the stipe. This tissue in called the *Veil.* As the cap expands this tissue breaks away, some portion remaining attached to the margin of the cap, while the other may form a ring on the stipe which is termed as the *Annulus.* It is very delicate and can easily be rubbed off or may even be washed away by rains.

The stipe or stalk

The stalk supporting the pileus is also known as stipe. Its presence or absence and mode of its attachment to the cap is an important character for identification of genera. Mostly the stem is centrally attached to the cap, but in some cases the attachment may not be exactly in the middle but lateral, then it is known as *Eccentric.* The stem may be solid, fleshy throughout or may be hollow in which the central cavity is stuffed with pithy substances. In shape the stem can be cylindrical, i.e., having the same diameter throughout, spindle shaped, being swollen in the middle and tapering towards both the extremities, or club shaped when it enlarges towards the top and tapers towards the base into a root-like form. The *Bulbous* stipe is that in which the base shows a sudden enlargement whereas in *Marginate* the stipe base widens into a sort of saucer with a well-defined margin.

Volva (universal veil)

Initially the entire fruit body prior to differentiation is covered by a universal veil. As the carpophore extends, this veil breaks and remains as a cup 'Volva' surrounding the base of the stipe. Or some portion of the entire veil tissue may remain as scales or marks on the expanded pileus.

According to the presence or absence of annulus and volva, the mushrooms can be put in the following four categories : (1) the mushroom in which both annulus and volva present as in *Amanita;* (2) only annulus is present and volva is absent, e.g., *Agaricus;* (3) in which only volva is present and annulus is absent as in *Voivariella;* and (4) in which both annulus and volva are absent, e.g., the common fairy ring (*Marasmius oreades*).

Chapter 6

Cultivation of White Button Mushroom (*Agaricus bisporus*)

Agaricus bisporus can be grown anywhere if the essential conditions are obtained or controlled. These conditions are: temperature, moisture, ventilation, and good spawn.

Temperature

The temperature requirement for the spread of the mycelium or vegetative growth is 22–25°C. For the reproductive stage or fructification; the temperature requirement is 14–18°C. Within the limits prescribed, the temperature should be uniform throughout the growth of the crop. If it is too cold the development of the spawn will be retarded or arrested. A high temperature will favour the development of moulds and bacteria, which will soon destroy the spawn or crop.

Moisture

Moisture is an important factor in the cultivation of the mushroom and needs careful application. The mushroom requires an atmosphere nearly saturated with moisture, yet the direct application of water on the beds is more or less injurious to the growing crop. They should be protected from a dry atmosphere or spring drought. When watering becomes necessary it should be applied in a fine spray around the beds with a view to restore the moisture in the atmosphere.

Ventilation

Good aeration is essential for a healthy crop, as ventilation is one of the important factors governing mushroom production. Ventilation is responsible for the maintenance of congenial environmental conditions and also for the removal of toxic gas by the introduction of adequate fresh air. The information available indicates that the CO_2 level of 0.10 to 0.15 per cent volume is necessary during crop production and this can be achieved by giving 4 to 6 air changes/hour or introducing 10 cubic ft fresh air/sq ft bed area/hour. van Soest (1977) gave a rule of thumb formula, i.e., at a bed temperature of 16°C, one cubic metre of fresh air per hour per square metre of bed area for every kilogram of mushroom produced. Every degree centigrade increase in bed temperature above 16°C increases the production of CO_2 by about 25 per cent. This implies that the number of air changes must be increased by 20 per cent. However, drought must be avoided as it will cause rapid desiccation and the beds will also be affected.

Good spawn

Spawn is merely mycelium from a selected mushroom grown on some convenient medium and it is the strain of mushroom selected which decides the type of mushroom the spawn will produce. The essential qualities of good spawn are:

a) It should be of a strain originating from a single specimen of a perfect crop.

b) It should have the following aspects: The substratum must be covered with the white mycelium, it must be uniform and at the moment of removal from the container, should be absolutely free not only from mould but also from all other microorganisms. Although some of these characters may be visible at a glance, a good spawn cannot in principle be distinguished from bad spawn merely by looking at it. Sometimes odour may help to remove the suspicion. Fresh spawn has a strong mushroom odour, dried spawn is odourless. But only a thorough examination and test can establish whether the spawn is good or bad.

Suitable growing space

Mushrooms may be grown successfully in a variety of places. Commercial and amateur mushroom growing is done indoors.

The following space requirements are necessary for successful production:

1) The location should be easily accessible so that the manure and casing soil can be brought in and removed with ease.

2) The room should be well ventilated.

3) No direct sunlight should fall on the bed. Diffuse light however, will not harm mushroom growing.

4) The room temperature should not exceed 20°C during the growing period.

5) Heating facilities should be provided so that the room may be heated when the temperature drops low.

6) The location should have sufficient protection and insulation so that it is not subjected to sudden fluctuations in temperature, since mushrooms cannot withstand sudden changes in temperature.

7) Location for growing mushrooms should not be too moist. The idea has gained ground that mushroom should be grown in humid, badly ventilated rooms. This is an entirely wrong notion. Mushroom does not develop well in too high humidity and will not develop at all with insufficient ventilation.

8) The best way would be if each unit is filled at one time and is arranged so that it can be closed up tightly and completely isolated from its surroundings, in order to facilitate the fumigation and disinfection of the beds.

9) Near the location of mushroom growing, there should be good fresh water supply, availability of the fertilisers for making compost and a good market for the disposal of the mushroom.

Mushrooms have been grown successfully in cellars, garages and in any abandoned room. For the cultivation of white button mushroom (*Agaricus bisporus*) the following steps should be adopted.

i) Compost and methods of composting
ii) Spawn and methods of spawning
iii) Casing
iv) Harvesting

Compost and Methods of Composting

Compost is the substrate on which mushroom grows. The biochemical activities of a number of microorganisms make the substrate selective for the growth of mushroom, *A. bisporus.* The process of compost making is known as *Composting.*

Composting is defined as indefinite microbial degradation of organic wastes. These wastes include vegetable and animal matter, forest litter, remains of stubbles and roots in the soil, green manure, straw, household garbage, sewage sludge, animal manure, etc. The process of composting involves microbial proteins and conditioning of the fibrous material to absorb and retain moisture. In addition, the microorganisms change the physical properties of compost and make the growth of the competitive microorganisms more difficult.

The quality of the mushroom compost depends on:

1) nature and quality of basic materials,

2) organic and inorganic supplements and
3) management of the compost during composting.

Nature and quality of the basic material

Compost making with horse manure and its straw bedding is the most conventional method adopted by commercial growers. Horse manure, bedding (straw) and urine form the most balanced medium for rapid decomposition and do not need any supplementation for making good compost. Some horse manure compost also needs supplementation to make good compost when it is collected from a cleaned stable; where it does not receive a major part of the urine, an addition of small amount of inorganic nitrogen will give better result. In case of the manure with less bedding, addition of straw provides good physical condition to the compost and makes a better substrate for the growth of *Agaricus bisporus.* Keeping these elementary principles in mind, one can proceed to make good compost for *A. bisporus.*

According to Atkins (1974) horse manure is the best substrate although the manure of mules is as good as that of horses. He could not find cow manure had any advantage over horse manure. One-third manure of well-fed cattle with two-third horse manure worked very well. Peat moss mixed with loam used as bedding of horses was an acceptable supplement to the horse manure.

In cattle manure the problem is of high variability of the raw material used as cattle feed. The important factors are the proportion of straw in the manure, its moisture content, age, method of collection and storage. Old, heavy weight manures are valueless for composting as they are considerably decomposed and have lost the ability to heat up. Relatively fresh cattle manure in which the straw still retained its original colour to a large extent proved to be very satisfactory for composting. The very strawy manure does not compost properly and remains tough and spongy, whereas the strawless manure makes a very compact heap, having large anaerobic zones, intermediate manure can be used. In cattle manure nothing except gypsum should be added.

Since horse manure is becoming scarce, attempts have been made to find suitable substitutes. In order to produce an economical and competitive artificial manure or "synthetic" compost, industrial wastes and agricultural byproducts can be used. There are few factors which should be kept in mind for selecting a substitute for horse manure:

i) The composting period of the substitute should be the same or lower than the horse manure

ii) It should be easily available to the growers and at competitive rates as the horse manure

iii) Its production capacity should be equal or better than horse manure.

Several workers have studied the possibility of wheat straw, barley straw, rice straw, rye or oat straw, maize stem, corn cobs, etc. mixed with organic and inorganic supplements as a replacement for making the synthetic compost (Lambert, 1929; Sinden, 1949; Stoller, 1943; Edwards, 1949; Randle, 1969; Gerrit, 1974; Mantel *et al.*, 1972).

In preparing the compost from straw as the only plant residue many difficulties are faced. Mainly it is the slowness with which the straw gets wetted followed by delayed action of microorganisms. On wetting the straw, a sequence of microbial events is initiated. First a mixed flora (bacterial, actinomycetes and fungi) of mesophylic nature which grow and multiply below 40°C (104°F) increases in number. As the temperature of the pile increases, a thermophilic and thermotolerant flora which can grow and multiply at temperature above 40°C take over. This flora survives until peak heat is terminated by cooling, then there is again an increase in number of mesophilic organisms especially in long method of composting, Microorganisms make use of nitrogen and carbon for their metabolic activities. The energy required for this process is derived by aerobic and anaerobic decomposition. Wheat straw is mostly used for making the synthetic compost. In rice growing area rice straw is also used but the quantity of rice straw should be more as compared to wheat straw.

Barley straw can also be used for making the composts. This straw softens in shorter period during composting. The yield of mushroom is the same both in the case of wheat and barley straw, but the compost produced from the barley straw is much less.

Stoller (1943) reported that fibrous material like spent licorice roots (from which the licorice has been extracted) and spent tannery nuts, bark and leaves (byproducts after tanning extraction for industrial use) are even more satisfactory than straw. These materials already contain sufficient moisture, they are suitably decomposed and require only a short or no microbial decomposition.

After much experimentation on composting it has been found that a certain balance between cereal straw and a plant material in a green state can form an ideal mixture for the preparation of a mushroom compost. The green material, whether freshly harvested or dried, will hold the water and absorb the added water readily and will begin to undergo immediate decomposition. Temperature also rises rapidly and within a few days, the compost is ready. The green material supplies the microorganism with some of the nitrogen and the minerals which are required for the decomposition of the straw although sometimes additional inorganic salts are required, depending upon the nature of the material used and their relative concentration (Waksman and Renger, 1934) Compost with maize stem has been tried. In this case a year old well-preserved maize stem is cut into small pieces and mixed with wheat straw in the ratio of 2.5:1 on the basis of dry matter. The straw improves the structure of the material. About 1.2:1.5 parts of broiler manure is also added to enrich the nitrogen content of the compost. Compost with crushed corn cobs can also be prepared. Crushed corn cobs and wheat or rye straw in the ratio of 2 to 1.5 is the most ideal ratio. On the basis of dry matter, broiler manure can be used as a nitrogen supplement to corn cobs.

As an alternate to cereal straw, the primary ingredients for mushroom substrate can be vegetable material such as sugarcane bagasse, pulverised tree bark and wood waste.

Sawdust can also be used for making compost. Sawdust is advantageous over common compost material, as it does not require grinding and is uniform in composition, it is easy to mix and handle. Hard wood such as oak, birch, beech and maple is suitable for the purpose. The unsuitability of soft wood is due to the presence of resins and lignin.

Sewage sludge is a very desirable supplement for sawdust. It is dried and mixed thoroughly with the saw dust before composting. If the sludge is not dry but watery or diluted, only a small quantity can be added without making the sawdust too wet. If the sawdust is partially dried and pasty it is very difficult to mix. Sludge is a good source of microorganism and the microbial growth substances, which may be very helpful in composting. Sawdust compost if correctly made is a useful substitute for horse manure compost (Rampe, 1953; Block, 1965). The temperature in the sawdust does not go very high during composting but if sludge is added to the sawdust, then the temperature goes a little higher than where sludge is not mixed. The required temperature during composting can be attained with nitrogen supplement (Block and Rao, 1962).

Organic and inorganic supplements

In the preparation of synthetic compost the presence of nitrogen, phosphate and potassium in different ratio is essential. Deficiency of any one of these will cause reduction in yield. The number of sources hardly matter as long as they provide the desired ratio. The

C : N ratio plays the most important part and for good compost this ratio is about 17 : 1. The supplementation of organic matter for an optimum result varies as per the basic material.

Nitrogen supplementation is also a very important factor. Deficiency of nitrogen often limits the yield, but by increasing the nitrogen, the yield increases. Increase of nitrogen should be up to 3 per cent level of the finished compost at the time of spawning (Schisler and Sinden, 1962). During the early stages of composting, much of the nitrogen is ammonified and in later stages, the ammonia recombines with microbial protein which is a good nutrient for mushroom. Ammonia as such is very toxic to the mushroom (Stoller, 1945; Sinden and Hauser, 1953).

The amount of nitrogen supplement is calculated in such a way as to give 2 to 2.5 per cent total nitrogen content in the starting mixture. Organic nitrogenous sources are better than inorganic ones because they supply carbon, potassium, phosphorus and also have a better heating capacity. Organic nitrogenous material may be unsatisfactory sometimes due to the presence of toxic substances. The selection of the nitrogen source depends upon the cost of the material comparable to the yield of mushroom obtained. The supplementation of organic matter for good results varies as per the basic matter. In the case of inorganic nitrogenous substances like ammonium salt, cyanamide, and special precautions should be taken while nitrates may be used freely.

The poultry manure can be used to replace part of the organic nitrogen supplement and to give good yield. It also adds a significant amount of fine dry matter to the compost which helps to counteract the strawiness of the horse manure and improve the texture of the compost. For supplementation of the nitrogen source any other nitrogen-rich organic material can be used. The amount of organic matter and nitrogen have to be the same as in chicken manure. If less chicken manure is used, it is possible to apply urea or ammonium nitrate as nitrogen source but if the amount of chicken manure becomes too small, the yield is negatively affected because of the shortage of the available carbon source. The structure of the compost is very important and there should be definite dry matter, water, air ratio during composting in order to have an optimum heating of the compost (Gerrit, 1974). If the straw is very fine for synthetic compost, less chicken manure can be used.

In the case of fresh horse manure, increasing the amount of ammonium sulphate and calcium carbonate generally increases the yield, but the reverse is the case with old horse manure. Increasing the amount of ammonium sulphate delays the decomposition in the pile, while a very high amount completely stops the fermentation. Increasing the amount of calcium carbonate slackens down the decomposition but does not reduce the yield. The addition of a limited amount of ammonium sulphate shows faster decomposition. It is necessary to study the combination of ammonium sulphate and calcium carbonate thoroughly (Rasmussen, 1965). One should be careful to add the right type of supplement, as chicken manure does not increase the yield with the combination of ammonium sulphate and calcium carbonate though with cotton seed meal, it is more effective (Rasmussen, 1965). Similarly, ammonium sulphate with or without limestone does not give an increase in the nitrogen content of the compost but it increases the ammonia content which reduces the yield. Ammonia content above 0.3 per cent reduces the yield (Sinden and Schisler, 1962; Flegg, 1960 and Edwards, 1950). There is a highly significant correlation between nitrogen and yield for synthetic compost but not for natural compost; therefore, a nitrogen supplementation which increases nitrogen without any increase in ammonia contents is desirable (O' Donogue, 1965).

Supplementation would be much cheaper if the ammonia from a cheap nitrogen source such as sulphate of ammonia could be converted into microbial protein by the microbes. This can be possible with the addition of available carbohydrate to the compost (Hayes and Randle, 1969; Gerrit *et al.*, 1965). Most often organic nitrogen is used as an activator, ammonium nitrate is the basic inorganic nitrogen supplement. Urea is often used as a source of free NH_3 during composting.

The composting process must, therefore, be regulated to produce a high amount of protein and a minimum amount of ammonia. Cotton seed meal, wheat flour, dried skim milk, fish meal, gluten meal, linseed meal, soybean meal, malt sprouts, meat scraps, ground rye grain, cotton steep liquor, Brewer's grain, molasses, corn syrup, etc., were used by Schisler and Sinden (1962); Gerrit (1974); McCanna (1969) and Seth (1976). Out of all these sources, cotton seed meal gives the best results. It means that the plant concentrates having a high protein content give a greater increase in yield than the animal concentrates. Molasses encourage the growth of bacterial and other moulds and hence reduce the yield. The combination of cotton seed meal, molasses, flour, etc., with skim milk gives an increase in yield whereas no significant increase was observed when they were added separately or in combination with each other.

The increase in yield is not achieved by merely adding more nutrient but it is increased by adding that particular nutrient in which the compost is deficient. An addition of nutrient in an already balanced compost would not help to increase the yield. After a certain limit of supplementation there is no further increases in yield, it is perhaps due to the poor growth of either the composting microorganism or the mushroom mycelium itself. When a higher amount of supplement is added, sometimes heating occurs which affects the yield.

Management of the compost during composting

There are two main methods of composting—long method and short method. The long method takes about three to four weeks whereas composting by short method takes 12 days.

Long Method

The compost should be prepared on a well-cleaned, *pucca* and preferably cemented floor. It may be done either in the open or under a shed whose sides are open. If composting is done outside, then the heap should be protected from rains by covering it with a plastic sheet. If composting is done inside the room, then the room should be well ventilated.

There are two types of compost: (i) natural compost and (ii) synthetic compost.

Natural Compost: Natural compost is prepared from horse dung obtained from stables in which abundant wheat or barley straw has been used for bedding. It is desirable to add one-third the weight of wheat straw to the horse dung. It should never contain an admixture of dung from other animals but 100 to 110 kg chicken manure and 3 kg urea per tonne may be added. The dung must be fresh and must not have been exposed to rain. The manure as obtained from the stable in a damp condition is made into a heap 1 metre high. After 3 or 4 days, when the heap begins to steam due to fermentation and gives off an odour of ammonia, it is opened up. This is repeated 4 to 5 times at an interval of 3 to 4 days. Twenty-five kg gypsum per tonne of horse dung is added in two instalments at the second and third turning. At the final turning, nematicide is mixed in the manure (Kapoor and Bahl, 1982).

Synthetic Compost: The following ingredients are required (Kapoor and Bahl, 1982);

Wheat straw (chopped 8 to 20 cm long)	250 kg
Wheat bran	25 kg
Ammonium sulphate or calcium ammonium nitrate	4 kg
Urea	3 kg
Gypsum	20 kg

This will make compost to fill up about 15 to 16 trays.

Wheat straw is spread over a *pucca* floor and wetted thoroughly by sprinkling water (Fig. 6.1). Wheat bran and other ingredients except gypsum are mixed thoroughly in wet straw, which is finally stacked into a pile about 1 metre high and 1 metre wide. The heap is compressed by applying light pressure.

The heap with mixed ingredients can also be made with the help of the wooden mould. It has three wooden boards–one-end board and two-side boards. The side boards can be attached with the end board by clamps as shown in (Fig. 6.2a, b). The whole board is kept on the ground. The mixed compost ingredients are put in the mould and compressed slightly. The side boards are detached from the end board and are moved lengthwise, again the mixed ingredients are put in the mould, this way a long pile of the compost can be made (Fig. 6.3). The pile should not be pressed tightly otherwise anaerobic condition will set in. If a long heap is made then perforated pipes can be placed vertically in the heap for

Fig. 6.1. Wetting of Straw

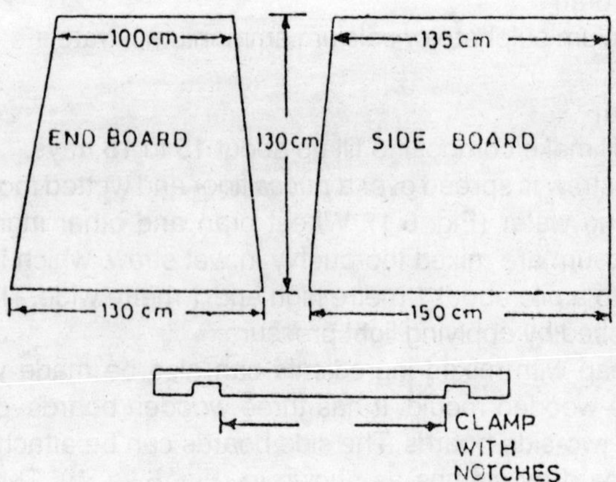

Fig. 6.2 (a). Wooden Board and Clamps for Making the Mould.

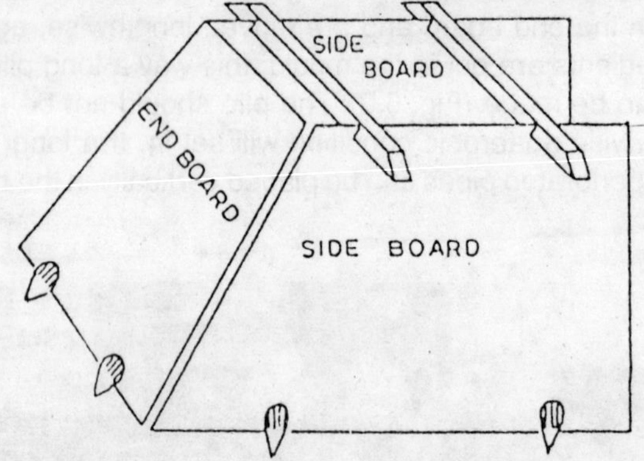

Fig. 6.2 (b). Assembled Mould for Making the Compost Heap.

aeration. It is essential to open the entire pile (Fig. 6.4) and re-do it a number of times according to the following schedule.

Stack the heap	0 day
1st turning	5th day
2nd turning	10th Day
3rd turning	14th day, add 10 kg gypsum
4th turning	18th day, add 10 kg gypsum
5th turning	22nd day, spray with 40 ml nemagon
Final turning	26th day, spray 10 ml melathion in 5 litre water

At each turning water should be sprinkled to make up the loss of water due to evaporation. The compost, when ready for spawn-

Fig. 6.3. Compost Heaps.

Fig. 6.4. Opening of Compost Heaps.

ing, is dark brown in colour and without any smell of ammonia and has sufficient moisture when pressed between the palm.

Many formulae have been given by different workers.

Formulae given by Indian Institute of Horticultural Research, Banglore:

Formula 1

Wheat straw (6 inch pieces) or	300 kg
Paddy straw	400 kg
Ammonium sulphate or calcium ammonium nitrate	9 kg
Superphosphate	9 kg
Urea	4 kg
Wheat bran	30 kg
Gypsum	12 kg
Calcium carbonate	10 kg

Straw must be kept wet for two days. When paddy straw is used add 6 kg cotton seed meal on the 4th turning. All fertilisers are broadcasted on moist straw before making the heap.

Formula 2

Paddy straw	150 kg
Maize stalk	150 kg
Ammonium sulphate	9 kg
Superphosphate	9 kg
Urea	4 kg
Rice bran	50 kg
Gypsum	12 kg
Calcium carbonate	10 kg
Cotton seed meal	5 kg

These two formulae are used for long methods of composting and schedule of turning is— days 0, 6, 10, 13, 16, 19, 22, 25, 26 (filling).

Formula 3

Horse manure	430 kg
Wheat straw	250 kg
Chicken manure	100 kg
Brewer's grain	30 kg
Urea	7 kg
Gypsum	20 kg

Formula 4

Wheat straw	300 kg
Chicken manure	120 kg
Rice bran	20.6 kg
Brewer's grain	22 kg
Urea	6 kg

Cotton seed meal	5 kg
Gypsum	10 kg

Formula 5

Wheat straw	1000 kg
Chicken manure	400 kg
Brewer's grain	72 kg
Urea	14.5 kg
Gypsum	30 kg

Formula 6

Paddy straw	3 ton
Chicken manure	1½ ton
Wheat bran	125 kg
Gypsum	90 kg

Formula given by Seth (1975)

Long method of composting

Wheat straw	1 ton
Calcium ammonium mitrate (CAN)	30 kg
Superphosphate	25 kg
Urea	12 kg
Sulphate of potash	10 kg
Wheat bran	100 kg
Molasses	16.6 litre
Gypsum	100 kg
Nemagon	266 ml

Turning schedule

0 day	Stack
1st turn	5th day (50 per cent nitrogen fertiliser)
2nd turn	7th day (molasses)
3rd turn	10th day (gypsum + nemagon and fill in the container)

It was allowed to remain in the container for 8 to 10 days. The temperatures in and outside compost as well as in the container ranged between 72 and 76°C.

Formulae given by Garcha (1981)

Formula 1

Wheat straw (Turi)	300 kg
Calcium ammonium nitrate (CAN)	9 kg
Urea	3 kg
Superphosphate	3 kg
Muriate of potash	3 kg
Wheat bran	15 kg
Molasses	5 kg
Gypsum	30 kg

Lindane dust or BHC (5 per cent)	250 kg
or	
Linotox	60 ml
Nemagon	30 ml

Formula 2

Wheat straw	300 kg
Poultry litter	60 kg
Calcium ammonium nitrate (CAN)	6 kg
Urea	2 kg
Superphosphate	3 kg
Muriate of potash	3 kg
Wheat bran	15 kg
Gypsum	30 kg
Lindane dust or BHC (5 per cent)	250 kg
or	
Linotox	60 ml
Nemagon	30 ml

Paddy straw can also be used instead of wheat straw. However, the equivalent of 300 kg of wheat straw should be 400 kg paddy straw. The other ingredients remain the same.

Formula given by the Srinagar laboratory

Wheat straw	300 kg
Molasses	12 kg
Urea	4.5 kg
Wheat bran	50 kg
Gypsum	12 kg
Muriate of potash	2 kg
Cotton seed meal	5 kg

Short Method

Described by Sinden and Hauser (1950), this composting has two phases.

Ingredients

Chopped wheat straw	1000 kg
Chicken manure	400 kg
Brewer's grain	72 kg
Urea	14.5 kg
Gypsum	30 kg

Phase I. Outdoor composting. Prestacking—four days

Brewer's grain and chicken manure are added to wheat straw. Sufficient water is added but there should be no leaching. The stack should be 3.3 × 2.5 × 1.0 metre. Give turning and make the stack of slightly smaller size (3 m × 2 m × 1 m). Straw is trampled with feet and watered if necessary.

0 day — Prepare heap in the usual way as in long composting. Add full quantity of urea and spray water if necessary.

Day 2 — Give first turning.

Day 4 — Give second turning and add full quantity of gypsum.

Day 6 — Give third turning.

Day 8 — Fill in trays for steam pasteurisation.

The pH of compost should be 8.5. In case it has less nitrogen supplementation should be done but the nitrogen should not exceed 2 per cent of the dry weight.

Phase II. It has two main purposes.

1) Conversion of ammonia into microbial protein.

2) Pasteurisation—Killing of microorganisms which are competitors and to make the substrate suitable only for *Agaricus bisporus.*

Phase II can be completed either by steam heat or fumigation with methyl bromide.

Steam pasteurisation: Initially live steam or dry heat is introduced to raise both air and compost temperature and then fresh air is introduced to establish anaerobic fermentation. For this phase the temperature should be between 52 and 60°C in the compost. There should be free circulation of moist air around the beds and oxygen supply should be between 15 and 20 per cent. For these conditions a well-insulated room is required. Trays evenly filled with compost are stacked in a pre-warmed room as quickly as possible to avoid heat losses. Sufficient space is kept between the trays to allow the free movement cf the air. All ventilators and doors are closed. Live steam is introduced to raise the temperature of compost up to 52 to 54°C. This temperature is maintained for 2 to 4 days. After that, the temperature of the compost is further raised to 58 to 60°C for 4 hours. The steam supply is shut off and fresh air is introduced slowly and gradually by controlling the ventilation system to lower the temperature of the tray beds (2 to 3°C per 24 hours). The temperature of the bed is lowered to 52 to 54°C and the same temperature is maintained for 4 days. By this time ammonia completely disappears from the compost and the temperature is further lowered to 24°C. Now it is ready for spawning. Fresh air circulation is essential throughout phase II to equalise the temperature and to supply oxygen to every part of the compost. Lack of oxygen in phase II reduces the thermogenesis within the compost. If with sufficient oxygen supply there is a weak thermogenesis it shows that the phase I condition was extended too long or the condition of phase I was not proper.

In phase II, if the ammonia smell persists for more than 60 to 72 hours it denotes that the composting process was not correct or excess of nitrogen was added in the beginning. Sometimes the air temperature is raised to 55 to 60°C to kill the insects and spores of competitors. This process is done at the end of phase II when active thermogenesis is completed otherwise there will be overheating of the compost. Phase II ends abruptly with a rapid decline of temperature to 25°C. Spawning is done immediately.

A compost fermentation method by means of forced air circulation

This method was devised by Neng Shieh (1981). This is actually a process of outdoor composting with indoor pasteurisation.

Fermentation Chamber for Compost

A hollow double-sheet plastic cloth sealed all the edges by heat. The plastic cloth has to exclude ultraviolet light. Redmud plastic is used in this experiment. Once the air is sent to the compost centre and flown out into chamber, space increasing its pressure within, and the hollow air pack is filled up with air, it becomes immediately a fermentation chamber of compost.

Formulation of Compost

By the conventional method in Taiwan, the compost has been made from rice straw and some chemicals with a ratio by weight as follows:

Rice straw	100
Urea	1
Ammonium sulphate	2
Calcium superphosphate	2
Calcium carbonate	2
Lime	2
Water	200

Process of Composting and Fermentation

Rice straw was cut to 10–12 cm before adding the lime solution for preparing the stack. Two days later all chemicals described above are added, and the proper amount of water is given, for the stacking. When the first turning is done on fourth day after stacking, the turned compost is put on the plastic film prepared on the ground. An air duct is laid across under the centre of compost and connected to a blower. Then everything is covered with the specific double-sheet plastic cloth. When the blower starts, the air is sent through the air duct to the compost centre and it flows out into the chamber space increasing gradually its air pressure within. Eventually, the plastic cloth becomes an arch-shaped fermentation chamber. The air inside is returned to the blower's inlet by forced circulation continuously. On one hand, a small amount of fresh air is provided, on the other hand, the exhausted air is led into the air pack between the double plastic layers before being discharged into the open air. This is to maintain the temperature in the fermentation chamber. During the endless air circulation, the compost temperature rises gradually until it reaches the designated temperature. There is no need of extra heating. The whole process takes about 10–12 days.

Mechanical composting

Barrel composting is a type of mechanical composting. A method of barrel composting is devised by Baker and Baker (1981) is as follows: The octagon-shaped barrel is 16m long and 3.8m across, with five circular steel bands spaced along its length on the outside. The support frame is made of steel, with the eight flat surfaces of marine ply. Barrel capacity of 40 tonnes is sufficient to produce compost for 55m^2 of cropping areas.

Power is supplied by 5.6 kW motors driving two hydraulic pumps, in turn to two hydraulic motors, each with gear boxes on inverted heavy duty Thornicraft differentials. The barrel is mounted on ex-aircraft tyres. Speed is variable from one revolution per hour to one revolution per minute. Normal operating speed is one revolution every eight minutes.

Air system: A unique air system features ducting built within the structure of the barrel, consisting of vented plywood plates across each corner of the octagon. The pressurised air distribution system runs the length of the barrel and is designed so that as the barrel revolves, air enters only from ducts along the base and is forced up through the compost.

Water: The water system consists of four main rails running the length of the barrel, with 12 misting nozzles along each rail. As the barrel revolves, only the top two rails at any time are in operation, discharging water at 280 kPa pressure. Water is stored in a 5000 L reservoir, which in winter is heated to 44°C.

Compost is based on wheat straw, requiring approximately 350 bales per fill. Activator ingredients consist of:

cattle manure
poultry manure

cotton seed meal
cotton seed hulls
gypsum
lime

with the aim of having a nitrogen content of 1.5 per cent entering peak heat. Materials are kept clean and dry and the manure screened to remove any objects that may damage equipment. Individual ingredients are measured and mixed in a concrete agitator for transport and dispensing at the point of filling the barrel.

Loading the Barrel

Straw is pre-wetted in batches of five bales (each of 20 to 25 kg) for four minutes in a dip tank. Bales are allowed to drain, leaving them with approximately 50 per cent of total water requirements. They are then carried by an air operated lifting station on to a conveyor where the bale ties are cut and counted. As the straw moves along the conveyor it is mechanically loosened, then fed into a Gehl forage harvester which cuts it to 4 to 5 cm.

The cut straw enters a hopper where it is mixed with the activator at the rate of 55 L per bale, so that the activator adheres to the moist straw as it enters a blower, which lifts the mixture up and into the barrel.

Composting Cycle

Day 0 — after filling the barrel is closed and rotated for 45 to 60 minutes so that the compost is levelled and mixed; at the same time 5000 L of water is added.

Day 1 — 1600 L of water is added and the compost is rolled and steamed for eight hours. Steam is introduced through the water system.

Day 2 — all water jets are removed, their spray patterns checked and cleaned if necessary. 50 kg of ammonium nitrate (34 per cent nitrogen) dissolved in 2000 L of water is then added to the compost.

Day 3 to 6 — each morning 1600 L of water is added to the compost as it is rolled and aired. The compost is further rolled and aired each afternoon.

Day 7 — the moisture content of the compost is tested and adjusted to 70 to 72 per cent.

Day 8 — barrel emptied.

Four central hatches are opened and the barrel is rotated intermittently so that the compost falls from the hatches on to a drag elevator, to a transfer belt, then on to a filling belt.

Trays are fed along a conveyor underneath the barrel, filled, stacked and transferred to the peak heat room.

The barrel is not completely self-emptying, but only the last 500 to 600 kg of a total of 40 tonnes has to be emptied manually.

For composting by any method the size of the heap is a very important factor. If it is large, then the compactness will be less and aerobic conditions will be there. Penetration of the air is affected by the difference of the external and internal temperature and by the compactness of the pile material, i.e., in summer less ventilation is needed and the pile must be kept smaller with loose, long straw. The side must be trampled down to prevent free penetration of air, which would carry away the ammonia and lower the temperature.

In Barrel system air was forced through the compost for making an aerobic and uniform compost. The entire Phase I cycle from straw wetting to Phase II was eight days. This system was later abandoned because of cost and compost quality.

In the mid 1980's in Austria and in Switzerland traditional Phase I composting systems were developed. These farms were very similar and both were built enclosed for the purpose of highly controlling odour emissions. All aspects of composting were carried out indoors. All process, air streams were treated using a biofilters before discharge. Materials were moved around computer controlled robot cranes during pre-wetting, with Phase I being carried out in pressed block of compost with ventilation. Capital and operating costs for these farms were high resulted into closing of the farms.

Later, in 1980s, research was initiated in a number of different countries into bulk composting without an extreme thermophilic phase, Perrin and Gaze (1987); Gerrits (1987); Gerrits and Van Griensven (1990); Derikx *et al.* (1990). Miller *et al.* (1990). Guilliver *et al.* (1991); Harper *et al.* (1992) and Noble and Gaze (1994).

Generally, in the low temperature composting there was a short pasteurization phase at about 60°C for a few hours, and then about a week of composting at around 47°C. The lower temperature composting not only controls odour but also saves raw ingredients substantially and the fostering of the thermophilic fungi populations which make compost selective and promote mushroom growth (Ross and Harris, 1983).

In general, low temperature methods did not produce compost equivalent to traditional methods, as these materials had poorer bulk densities and produced lower yields per bed surface area. In commercial practice, Vestizens (1994) found low temperature Phase I composts gave poorer yields and were less selective than enclosed composting methods having a high temperature (around

80°C) phase, Miller *et al.* (1990) found selectivity to be excellent in their low temperature composts reported for tunnels using pull nets, where the nets could interfere with uniform air flow. In commercial practice Gulliver *et al.* (1991) found enclosed high and low temperature Phase I compost to be the same in terms of yields, and that both enclosed methods were inferior to traditional methods.

In the past few years, commercial enclosed composting tends to follow the Italian practice of high temperature Phase I followed by a fairly standard Phase II in tunnels. Laborde *et al.* (1993) worked on enclosed composting which is in recent practice. Utility of bunker enclosed Phase I, with zones of high and lower temperature has been demonstrated by Overstijns (1994). Modifications in enclosed composting done by different workers made commercial growing successful.

Very high composting temperature of around 80°C tend to kill most microbes within compost, including all of the fungi and actinomycetes and most of the bacteria (Evered *et al.* 1995; Miller, 1996). Phase I tunnels can allow temperatures throughout the composting mass to become uniformly hot enough to eliminate populations required to complete Phase II. Currently three strategies are being used to deal with this problem. Materials from Phase I tunnels can be re-inoculated at the beginning of Phase II, Ventilation can be used in the tunnel cooler than 60°C thereby maintain desired population 5 to 10% of the material. Phase I can also be carried out in a bunker where the top and side layers of the compost will loose sufficient heat to prevent the entire composting mass to reach very high temperatures, and this cooler compost is then remixed with the hotter compost as an inoculant on removal of the compost from the bunker.

It is better to have the basic ideas of ideal composting to enable to have the better results in enclosed methods of composting. According to Miller (1994) the goals to be achieved in compost, ready for spawn run and cropping includes are:

1. Suitable bulk density i.e., wet weight bulk density of an approximately 550 to 600 kgm^3, related to straw softening and other structural charges.
2. Modification of plant materials so that nutrients are made available to the mushroom crop.
3. Biological removal of readily available initial nutrients to avoid overheating and competitor growth either Phase II or spawn run.
4. Building up of an appropriate bio-mass and a variety of microbial products, some of these can serve as a nutrient source for the mushroom.

5. Establishment of selectivity, i.e., the composting promotes the growth of *Agaricus* over competitor organisms. Selectivity is based on nutrition, structure, and other factors.
6. Modification of compost structure, so that it holds more water within the straw.
7. Building up of compost moisture content to serve as a water reservior for the mushroom crop.
8. Conversion for nitrogen into stable organic forms, making nitrogen available to *Agaricus* but not prone to further ammonification by competitors.

Selection of Enclosed Composting: Method of enclosed composting is determined according to the site. In Western Europe where composting yards are very large, odour and ammonia emission should be controlled. Phase I is carried out in completely enclosed tunnels and process air is treated by air washers and biofilters before discharge. The places where the rules on atmospheric emissions are not very strict, bunker systems are appropriate, while open bunker systems will permit some emissions to the atmosphere odour will be less compared to the conventional open air composting. Places, where adverse weather conditions exist and make traditional composting difficult enclosed Phase I system should be followed.

Enclosure should be decided in local community depending on economies and local community standards. Enclosed Phase I methods can save money in the areas of lower raw material losses, smaller land requirements, shorter process duration, lower labour cost and consistency of mushroom production.

Bunker systems rely on keeping outer zones of the compost cool enough (less than 60°C) so that thermophilic fungi and actinomycetes which are important to Phase II are not killed. For this, retaining walls should not be heavily insulated as some level of ambient airflow across the top of composting mass is required. Bunker system will cost less than a tunnel system.

Tunnel systems which achieve uniformly high temperatures require the compost to be re-inoculated with beneficial micro-organisms, so that Phass II can be carried out (Straatsma and Samson 1993; Straatsma *et al.* 1994). In commercial practice, inoculation of the Finished Phase I material is made with a finished Phase II compost. At this time, inoculants for high temperature Phase I materials are in the development stage.

Commercially, in bunker system about 25% of the Phase I composting mass should be maintained below 60°C, so that remixing the entire mass at the start of Phase II will provide sufficient self-inoculation to the remainder of the compost. This mixing of re-inoculation gives the variable result as compared to using a specific inoculant. Better process monitoring and control of the bunker Phase I might allow better and more consistent development of populations suitable for self-inoculation during the Phase I process.

The practice of enclosed composting is becoming popular, improvement will further make the mushroom growing more successful. While low temperature single phase methods of preparing compost can be used to grow mushrooms. High temperature Phase I appears to be more advantageous in producing high yielding commercial composts.

Futher research towards enclosed composting with environmental control may cost less than the traditional method of composting in future.

It is necessary to chop the straw in order to facilitate the retention of heat and moisture both during the composting period and during the sweating out process. Chopped straw is also easier to handle. Long straw binds and is laborious to mix. Chopped straw compost is better than straw which is partially chopped or not chopped at all. The length of the composting period is influenced: (i) by the nature and subdivision of the fibrous material, and (ii) by the aeration of the compost pile. The size of the pile also affects the composting and accordingly the yield. The smaller piles have a relatively large surface exposure to the atmosphere, so that almost all parts of the piles receive good aeration, reverse was the condition in the case of a large pile. Good aeration is also obtained by placing a ventilatory in the centre of the large pile. When preparing the compost with straw it is necessary to compress the straw in order to prevent too much aeration from drying out and cooling in the straw compost, whereas with closely packed material it is necessary to make special provision for aeration. When good aeration is provided manure can be composted in seven days (Stoller, 1943). The CO_2 concentration at a point in the pile is more dependent on the width of the pile than the height.

During composting, moisture is also very important. If the chemical composition of a compost is good, the course of the composting process depends upon the dry matter, water, and air ratio in the compost (Gerrits, 1974). This ratio is highly dependent upon the moisture content and the force with which the compost is compressed.

If moisture is low during composting, bacterial decomposition is arrested and nitrogen escapes as ammonia and other volatile forms of nitrogen. At a very high moisture level, unaerobic conditions set in and bring down the speed of the decomposition. Depending upon the nature of the composting material the moisture level can be adjusted. If the compost is wet (more than 70 per cent) there is a low supply of oxygen. Due to the slow activity of microorganisms the temperature rises slowly and with the short supply of oxygen the anaerobic condition will set in and carbon dioxide will be more. If such condition is obtained in the larger part of the pile the quality of the dry matter will be affected. The oxygen concentration in the heap has a great influence on the liberation and fixation of ammonia. The optimum moisture content at which the mycelium grows best is 68–70 per cent. If the compost is very dry (less than 60 per cent) at spawning the mycelium growth is very thin.

The interval between the turns is also important and is governed by the nature of the material. The object is to turn as soon as there is a risk of an anaerobic area development. The length of the composting period is very important although the determination of the length is an art. The experienced grower considers the composting is complete when the manure has a dark colour and when the tensile strength of the straw in the manure is low (indicating that the straw can absorb and retain water).

For a lay person the compost is ready when it has the following qualities:

a) The heap should have a light brown appearance.

b) The straw should be neither too long nor too short.

c) The heap should have lost the smell of ammonia and have a rich mushroom aroma.

d) When squeezed tightly in the hand the moisture should be released in the form of only a little dampness and the compost fragments should only just bind together.

The quality of a mushroom compost depends on:

a) The nature and quality of the basic material.

b) Organic and inorganic supplements.

c) The management of the compost during the composting period.

Spawn and Methods of Spawning

Spawn is the mushroom seed, comparable to the vegetative seed in crop plants. It is merely the vegetative mycelium from a selected mushroom grown in a convenient medium and the particular strain of mushroom selected, decides the type of mushroom the spawn would produce (Kligman, 1950). The success of mushroom cultivation and its yield depend to a large extent on the purity and quality of the spawn used. In the seventeenth century when mushroom growing started, mushroom growers used to plant horse manure beds with horse droppings containing living mycelium which they called "spawn". Given here are some of the many improvements that have been done in spawn making from time to time.

1) *Virgin Spawn:* When the spores of the mushroom fungus fall on suitable substrate and the environment is also suitable, they germinate and form a mat of mycelium. This is dug out and used as spawn, and is known as "Virgin spawn". This type of spawn was used in France and exported to other countries (Atkinson, 1961).

2) *Flake Spawn:* When the beds are fully covered with mycelium before a crop of mushroom appears, the compost is collected, broken, dried and used fresh to inoculate other new beds. This type of spawn is called flake spawn.

3) *Brick Spawn:* A mass consisting of horse and cow dung manure and loam is mixed with water, tapped out in a layer two inches thick and cut into pieces when half dry. These pieces are then inoculated with the old spawn by making a hole in each, and after the spawn grows through the entire piece, it is dried and sold as brick spawn. Mycelium from tissue cultures is inoculated into the bricks and thus a vastly improved laboratory type of brick spawn is prepared.

The inoculum for the aforementioned spawns were prepared by inoculating specially prepared bottles of sterilised horse manure, tobacco stem or other medium with the germinated spores of the mushroom. However, these spawns are not in use at present.

4) *Grain Spawn:* Another type of spawn that has been developed is, spawn using grain (wheat or rye) as a base. The grain spawn is now almost universally used. The larger grains carry a greater reserve of food material per grain for mushroom mycelium so the spawn prepared with larger grains can withstand adverse conditions such as poor composting, etc. The small grains provide more points of inoculum per gram of spawn, so the spawn prepared with smaller grains will cover the compost sooner.

Different workers reported different grains for making grain spawn. Stoller (1962) preferred rye grain to sorghum for avoiding sectoring and advised the use of 6 g of gypsum and 1.5 g chalk per pound of grain to avoid the clumping of grains. Stoller (1968) got a faster growth of mycelium on hulled grain and cotton seed meal while buck wheat and wheat bran showed poor growth. San Antonio and Hwang (1971) advised that cereal grain can be the only common substrate for commercial spawn production. Munjal (1973) recommended the use of jowar grain for the preparation of *Agaricus bisporus* spawn. Kumar *et al.* (1975), reported that jowar gave better growth of mycelium after mixing 2 per cent gypsum and 6 per cent $CaCO_3$ with the boiled grain by weight. Hu and Lin (1972) used shell powder, starch, compost powder and grain hull powder for making granular spawn in Taiwan.

Advantages of grain spawn

a) It is easier to plant than manure spawn, especially in the tray system where for spawning it can be scattered over the surface without unstacking and restacking the tray. Thus labour is saved. With the standard shelves system, it is usually planted in the compost because of the quicker drying out of the compost surface layer as compared with the tray system of growing.

b) Grain spawn run is faster and growers can save a few days for starting production.

Disadvantages of grain spawn

a) Due to its susceptibility to green moulds, the beds cannot be spawned at as high a temperature as with manure spawn.

b) It does not ship well and cannot be kept by the growers once it has been removed from the culture container.

c) Grain spawn cannot be kept for any length of time in cold storage.

d) Rats and mice dig up the beds to get the grain.

e) It is not as resistant to adverse conditions as are the other types.

Methods of preparation of grain spawn

a) *Agaricus bisporus*

Sorghum, wheat or bajra grain can be used for making spawn. The grain should not be very old, or broken, insecticide or fungicide treated or insect damaged. The grain is boiled with an equal volume of water till the water dries out. The grain should become soft but it should not get split or allow the starch to ooze out. If there is excess of water it should be drained off. The grain should be spread over alkathene sheets and left for some time then mixed thoroughly with calcium carbonate @ 8 per cent by the grain weight. The mixture is filled in a wide mouthed bottle, plugged tightly and sterilised for two consecutive days at 15 lbs p.s.i. for half an hour. Calcium carbonate absorbs excess of water and thus helps in keeping the grain separate. It also helps to maintain the pH. After 2 days of sterilisation the bottles are inoculated with the culture of mushroom and incubated at 25 ± 1°C for 3 weeks. By this time, the grains become covered with white mycelium. The combination of 2 per cent gypsum and 6 per cent lime by grain weight gives the best results in the process of making grain spawn for *Agaricus bisporus* (Fig. 6.5)

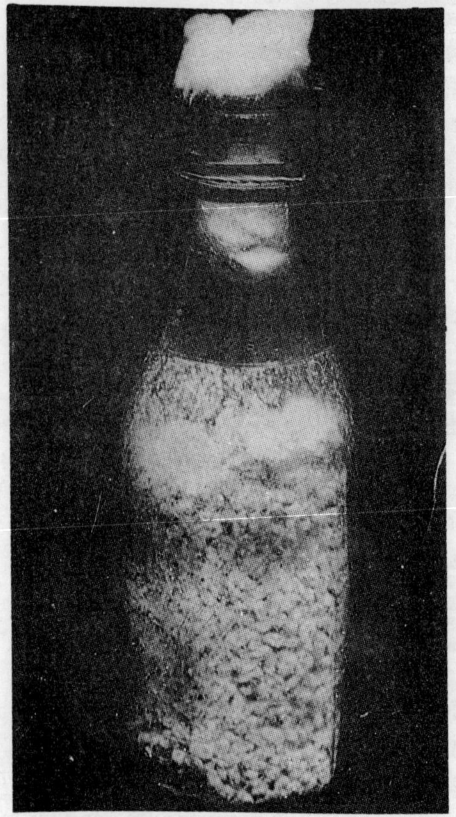

Fig. 6.5. Grain Spawn in Bottle.

b) *Volvariella volvacea*

The spawn of paddy straw mushroom can be prepared in a way similar to that of *Agaricus bisporus.* The spawn can be prepared on paddy straw also. In this case paddy straw is cut into pieces of 4 to 6 cm and soaked in water overnight. The straw should be completely dipped in water. Excess water is drained off and 10 per cent of arhar dal powder or gram dal powder is mixed by weight of wet straw. Three-fourth of the bottles are filled with the mixture, plugged tightly and sterilised for two consecutive days at 15 lbs p.s.i. for half an hour, inoculated with the *Volvariella* culture and incubated at

32 ± 2°C for 10 days. The mycelium spreads in fortnight and bright coloured chlamydospores start appearing.

The highly desirable qualities for selecting good mushroom spawn are as follows:

i) High yielding capacity: A good strain must be selected for the purpose. The strains are isolated either from the mushroom tissue, preferably from the junction of the stipe with the pileus or from the spores. In either case, the fruit body itself should have the desirable characteristics and must be taken from the first or second flush. A strain with silky creeping growth is considered better than that with a fluffy growth or the culture in which the sectoring does not occur. It is found that the master cultures lose their viability after sometime and hence need to be checked and stored in a refrigerator (below 4°C). It is also useful to transfer the master culture on different media, so that the nutritional deficiency of the media can be made up. In the case of *Volvariella* the mycelial growth is more profuse and small brick-coloured knots (chlamydospores) appear afterwards. It has been observed that the more the number of knots the higher is the yield. The substrate on which spawn is made also affects production.

ii) The medium should be well covered with a heavy growth of spawn.

iii) The spawn should be free from mould contamination.

iv) The spawn should be of a well-selected strain that has been thoroughly tested.

Factors determining the amount of spawn needed

The amount of spawn used should be sufficient to help rapid and vigorous coverage of the beds with the organism. It must be sufficient, to fight successfully against any other organism that are always present in manure and to overcome any slightly adverse conditions of moisture or consistency that are present. The amount of inoculum which an individual spawn piece will give depends on the exposed surface that comes in contact with the manure. When conditions are ideal in the beds, less spawn is needed. It is up to the grower to decide the amount of spawn needed within the foregoing limits. A good inoculation of spawn is protection against adverse conditions.

Method of spawing

Methods of spawning are known to affect the yield of mushrooms:

1) *Double layer spawning*: In this, spawning is done by scattering the spawn on tray beds when half-filled with compost and then

after the complete filling of the tray. The spawn is gently pressed with the forefinger uniformly each time and trays are covered with newspaper sheets.

2) *Top spawning*: After filling the trays up to the brim with compost, the spawn is planted just above the surface and then a thin layer of compost is spread out because if the spawn is at the top of the compost it dries up quickly. If one is certain that the top will not dry out it will not be necessary to plant the spawn deep, if the compost is wet it is advisable not to go deep.

3) *Through spawning*: The whole of the spawn grain or shredded manure spawn are mixed throughout the compost.

4) *Shake-up spawning*: A few workers have reported a better yield by shake-up spawning. After one week of spawning the compost is thoroughly shaken up, and replaced in the shelves or in trays. After that either it is cased at once or a few days later.

5) *Active mycelium spawning*: This method has been developed in Germany. In this case fully run trays of spawned compost are used for spawning further trays. Thus one such tray is used for several trays. In this method, however, chances of contamination are more.

6) *Spot spawning*: The grain spawn can be put in the holes at a certain distance with a pointed stick or fingers. It is immaterial how the hole is made but care should be taken to ensure close contact of the inoculum with the surrounding compost to ensure a quick development of the mycelial strands. The cavity is covered with the compost.

7) *Super spawning*: Fresh pasteurised trays are planted as usual. This is referred to as preliminary spawning. After two weeks the compost from each tray is mixed with the compost from newly pasteurised trays and is packed firmly. This is known as super spawning.

Spawning the beds is of major importance, for all previous preparations, however carefully carried out, may represent capital and time lost, if the operation is done carelessly. Rasmussen (1961) while comparing top spawning, shake up and super spawning found that the lowest yield was obtained from top spawning and the highest yield was obtained from the super spawning method. Flegg *et al.* (1966), reported that there was not much difference in yield with regard to the method of spawning whether it was spot, surface, active mycelium or shake up spawning but there was a tendency for through spawning to give better yield.

Under Indian conditions Shandilya *el al.* (1974), tried spot, surface, through, spawn to spawn, shake-up and double-layer spawning and found that the through spawning method gave the highest yield followed by double-layer spawning. They also reported that spawn to spawn and shake-up spawning encouraged the development of competitive moulds and thus lead to reduction in yield. They got a better yield when the spawn run compost was added to the casing layer at the casing time and the pin head formation stage appeared within 9 days.

Storage of spawn

Different workers have different views regarding the storage of spawn. It is observed that the storage condition of spawn also affects its productivity. The productivity of spawn is reduced by 5, 6 and 8 per cent if the spawn is kept at 2°C for 68, 128 and 206 days respectively as reported by Heltay (1959) in the case of manure spawn. Stoller observed that spawn taken directly from the growing room grew faster than spawn kept at 2°C. Lemke (1968) reported that cream and white strains give different reactions regarding the storage of wheat grain spawn. Sengbusch (1968) could store the spawn of the cream variety for months at 20°C and white strains could be continued for 4 to 6 months storage at the same temperature. San Antonio and Hwang (1971) did not observe any reduction in yield of spawn of any variety, i.e., brown, cream or white, due to storage for 2 years.

The yield of *Pleurotus sajor caju* was almost the same from spawn kept for 2 months either at room temperature or in the refrigerator. The spawn kept in the refrigerator for 4 months did produce mushrooms, but the yield was less as compared to fresh spawn or spawn stored for a period of 2 months. Heltay and Barber (1959) also reported that spawn stored in the refrigerator (–2°C) for 2 to 4 months reduced the productivity of mushroom.

Arrangement of trays: (Figs. 6.6a, b) when the compost is ready it is filled in wooden trays of convenient size having four pegs on four corners, or it can be put on shelves. Spawning is done by any method described before. Spawned trays are covered with paper and are stacked one above the other as shown in Figs. 6.6a, b. Room temperature should be maintained at 22 to 25°C during the spawn run. Watering if necessary, should be done by spraying water on the paper (Fig 6.6a). Spawn run takes 10 to 15 days (Fig. 6.7).

Fig. 6.6 (a). Stacking of Mushroom Trays.

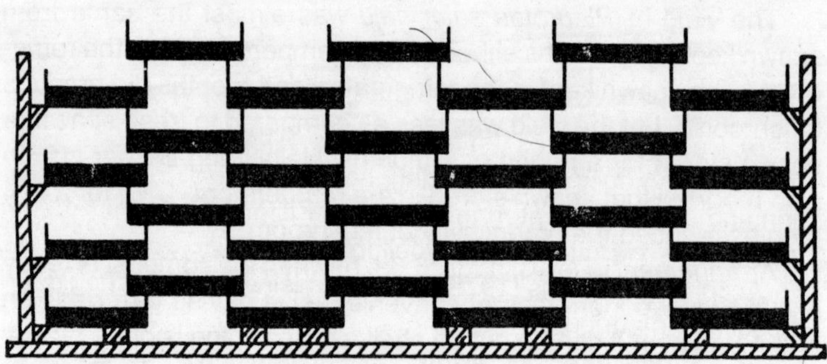

Fig. 6.6 (b). Stacking of Mushroom Trays.

Casing

Casing means covering the compost with a thin layer of soil or soil-like material after the spawn has spread in the compost (spawn run). Casing is done for the following reasons:

1) It gives support to the mushroom. Though mushroom forms in the uncased compost, it can fall due to its weight and the supply

Fig. 6.7. Spawn Run in Compost.

of food can be disrupted.

2) Casing soil provides humidity as it can hold water for a longer period.

3) It prevents quick drying of the spawned compost and therefore, it helps better spawn growth.

4) Vegetative mycelium is encouraged to fruit only when it enters into the medium which is deficient in nutrition. Casing soil provides such conditions.

5) Casing regulates the temperature. Sudden reduction of temperature also encourages fruiting, soil loses moisture by evaporation and after each watering a cool layer is provided which appear to shock the warmth loving mycelium into activity.

According to Atkins (1972) the ideal casing material should have the following attributes:

a) It should have good water holding capacity, otherwise water will go straight to the compost and the surface of the compost will become waterlogged and will cause damage to the spawn. It should absorb water quickly and should release it slowly.

b) It should have good aeration capacity, i.e., it should be quite porous so that exchange of gases can take place easily.

c) Its texture should not be altered by watering.

d) It should be neutral in reaction.

e) It should be free from disease organisms, insects and

undecomposed vegetable matter.

The French were the first to find that it is essential to cover compost with casing layer so as to induce a change in *Agaricus bisporus* from the vegetative phase to the reproductive phase. It is universally accepted now that for successful cropping, mushroom beds should be covered with a thin layer of casing soil. It is the belief of many workers that casing soil does not provide any nutrition but is valuable for its physical and chemical charcteristics. Structure and moisture holding properties are the primary physical factors influencing the yield and pH is the most critical chemical factor.

In France, powdered lime stone of the rock was used as casing material. Subsequently, soil became the common casing material. Many countries are using sphagnum peat as casing material.

Soil has been the universal casing material. Lambert (1929) found that heavy soil yielded better than sandy soil; clay, loam or even clay is also preferable when the physical conditions are such that they do not puddle or cake on the bed. It is a belief that casing soil of compact structure is unsuitable because it hampers the passage of air from compost to casing and *vice versa,* giving too high a concentration of carbon dioxide during fructification. Repeated watering throughout the cropping leads to even greater compactness and CO_2 concentration. Due to lack of free diffusion, the CO_2 concentration increases considerably thus affecting the yield adversely.

Lambert and Humfeld (1939) believed that clay soil is better than sandy soil provided, there is humus in it so that such soil does not pan too much during cultivation. If humus is lacking, the surface of casing soil is scratched at the end of the vegetative phase thus good flushes of mushroom may be obtained. Scratching of the top layer of casing soil provides better holding capacity. Steineck (1970) reported that a compact structure gives a better yield if the upper casing layer has a more airy structure. Stoller (1952) stated that compressed soil can hold more water and provides better contact with the compost layer. He found that pressing gave bigger, stouter and more solid mushrooms. Edward and Flegg (1953) found that the greater the number of pores in the soil, the better the diffusion and when more water was applied to the soil before casing, they found the yield was better. Lambert and Humfeld (1939) concluded that heavy clayish soil yielded better than lighter sandy soil.

Rao and Block (1962) found that equal parts of sand and peat as a casing mixture gives heavier fruiting. Last (1970) mentioned a casing mixture of loam, rotten dung and leaf manure to be applied immediately after spawning. In England, charcoal, sand, limestone, finely broken bricks and coarse washed ash were successfully used as a casing material. However, the additon of soil to the foresaid material gave increase in yield.

Now a days, actively growing spawned compost is mixed with the casing mixture and is believed that in such cases the fruiting is early.

In India, a number of mixtures have been recommended : (1) Well-rotten cow dung, mixed with light soil in the ratio of 3 : 1; (2) soil and sand ratio of 1 : 1; (3) farmyard manure and gravel ratio 4 : 1; (4) farmyard manure and loam ratio 1 : 1; (5) soil peat mixture 2 :1; (6) spent compost, sand and slaked lime (4 :1 :1) and nematicide mixture stacked in a pile (1.20 M × 1.0 M) in a shaded place and given 4 monthly turning. In case, the spent compost is pasteurised it is also treated with nematicide. The whole thing is decomposed within a year to a peaty black soil, which provides a good casing material. Kleermaker (1953) concluded that pH is more important than good structure of the soil and water holding capacity. Lambert and Humfeld (1939) concluded that neutral soil (pH 7) gave better yield than excessively acidic or alkaline soil. Some workers on the other hand noticed that pH of the casing soil between 8.0 and 8.5 are the most suitable for mushroom yield. Some reported that pH between 5.5 and 8.0 is suitable. The common practice among the growers is to adjust the pH between 7.0 and 7.5. The addition of lime to the casing mixture has an immediate effect of pH. It is also beneficial for the crop. Carbonate of lime or lime stone has been found to be the safest. Calcium has also been found to play an important role in fruit body formation. Bohuš (1959) said that casing material must also contain calcium.

Eger (1962) was the first to suggest that stimulus provided by the casing layer for sporophore formation is accelerated in the presence of microorganisms. *Pseudomonas putida* was found to be active in promoting the fruiting in *Agaricus bisporus* (Hayes, 1974). The activity of *P. putida* in casing soil is the result of environment created by the growing mycelium in the compost. It is suggested that *P. putida* releases iron which stimulates fructification. It was also found that there is a substantial increase in the number of pin heads and also fruit bodies by applying Ferrous salt to the casing soil. Flegg (1960) suggested that Manganese also increases the yield.

Sterilisation of casing soil

Soil contains many microorganisms. To use it as a casing material it should be sterilised in such a way that harmful micro-organisms are killed and the useful ones remain. Sterilisation of the casing material is done either by chemicals or by heating. Sterilisation may also be done by steam from boiler through perforated pipes and temperature raised to 60°C and maintained for 5 hours. Sterilisation under pressure is not advisable as the beneficial microorganisms are also killed and leave the soil more susceptible to re-infection.

Chemical sterilisation

Chemicals which are commonly used for sterilisation are formalin, chloropicrin, methyl bromide and vapam. For sterilisaion with formalin, about half a litre of formalin is diluted with 10 litres of water and used for 1 cubic metre of casing soil. The casing soil is spread over a plastic sheet and treated with formalin. The treated soil is piled up in a heap and covered with another plastic sheet for 48 hours. Later, the soil is uncovered and stirred frequently to remove the formalin fumes. This soil is fit for casing after about a week when it is free from the smell of formalin.

Time of casing

The time of application of casing is a controversial point. It may vary from 10 days to 3 weeks depending upon the spawning technique. Rasmussen (1970) indicated that early casing is successful but then watering, temperature and ventilation should be optimum during the prefruiting period for good results. Tschierpe (1973) mentioned that yield is reduced if casing is done too early or too late. When one should case is a difficult question to answer. Some believe that casing the bed as soon as one notices the spawn run properly, minimises the risks due to infection of the compost by airborne spores of moulds or other fungi as well as by the pests such as mushroom flies which burrow into the compost to lay their eggs.

Casing should be evenly done, otherwise where the casing soil is thin, mycelium will come up and stroma will be formed which will hinder pin formation. With uneven casing, watering will also be not uniform.

Thickness of the casing : 1 to 1.5" is found to be the most suitable thickness for the casing.

Cropping and Harvesting

Once spawn runned trays are covered with casing soil, the crop can be expected after 5 to 20 days. A fine spray of water should be given over the casing soil to maintain 70 to 80 per cent humidity. It is essential that fresh air should circulate over and around the boxes or tiers so that there should not be any pocket of carbon dioxide. Excessive humidity during the cropping will result in heavy concentration of carbon dioxide. The more the volume of mushrooms grown in a room the more will be the need of fresh air, as more carbon dioxide will be formed.

The greater the humidity and higher the temperature, the more are the chances of pests and diseases. It is, therefore, essential to keep the temperature low between 14 and 16°C. Apart from regular spraying of insecticides between flushes, efforts should be made to keep the circulation of fresh air around the beds. There should not be any unpleasant smell upon entering the mushroom house. The floor and walls should be frequently damped during warm weather which will prevent quick evaporation from the casing.

Mushrooms mostly appear in "Flushes" and at temperature of 68°F (15°C) it generally takes 7 to 8 days to come to the button stage from the first appearance of the formation of a pin head (Figs. 6.8 and 6.9). There is an interval of 8 to 10 days between the flushes. The humidity of the mushroom house will determine whether there is any need of watering the bed. If the atmosphere is dry then frequent watering is essential. While watering, it is necessary to give a gentle spray with a fine jet, otherwise the casing soil will get disturbed, panning of the surface will occur and the oxygen supply will be cut off.

After a few flushes one will find that the mushrooms are becoming lighter. This shows that the nutrients of the compost are getting exhausted. Though the mushrooms will be appearing in the beds there will not be heavy flushes later on. Therefore, a six-week crop is considered to be economical. When mushrooms have reached from the pin head to the button stage the question arises when the mushrooms should be plucked. It is a tricky question which is being asked by mushroom growers. There are no fixed days, stages or shapes of the mushroom. For the information of a lay person, however, the mushroom should be plucked when the cap is still tight over a short stem, or in other words, before the breaking of the veil. If the veil breaks then the colour of the gills will change to brown due to the formation of spores. The mushrooms will become leathery and will not be liked by the customer. It is also not advisable to pick very small mushrooms as in that case the weight of the individual mushroom will be less, and hence the yield will be low.

Mushrooms are plucked by twisting the mushrooms gently clockwise and anticlock-wise and afterwards it is pulled up very softly.

Fig. 6.8. Pins of Button Mushrooms Appearing in Trays.

Fig. 6.9. Mushrooms Growing on Shelves.

Along with the mushrooms, soil particles of the casing soil also come up clinging with the mycelial threads of the mushroom. The lower portion of the stipe is cut with a sharp knife and is put in the trash box. The cleaned mushrooms are collected in another box. If there are many pin heads around the mushroom which are to be plucked, then it is advisable to cut that mushroom with a sharp-edged knife, so that the nearby pins do not get disturbed. Otherwise those pin heads will not grow into buttons, and will turn yellow. Finally, many saprophytes may attack those dead pin heads and disease will spread. When all the mushroom of the desired size have been picked up, the next stage is to fill up the holes with a mixture of sterilised casing soil. The surface of the beds should be kept quite levelled and where new casing has been put this should be made firm by giving a gentle pat.

After picking and filling the holes the path of the mushroom house should be cleaned, before watering the trays. It is always advisable to water the trays after picking the mushrooms. If watering is done before plucking then the soil particle of the casing will stick to the cap of the mushroom and will spoil the whiteness of the mushroom.

The duration of cropping varies with circumstances. With the tray system a period of 6 to 7 weeks and in the case of the shelf system it varies between 6 and 12 weeks. Every grower should keep detailed cropping figures and periodically analyse them to determine the economic duration of his farm.

If there is an outbreak of disease and it is not controlled by the recommended treatment it is advisable to remove the diseased tray. The mushroom should be plucked very carefully and gently. All the processes from plucking to packing of the mushrooms should be done gently, otherwise bruises will occur on the cap of the mushroom and reduce its market value.

Diseases

Mushrooms are subject to many fungal, bacterial and viral disease. Even a little carelessness in different steps during cultivation can play havoc with the mushroom. Improper pasteurisation of compost and casing soil can be the major source of diseases. Once the disease is introduced in the farm the secondary infection can be carried out by different agencies, such as air, water, machines and workers. The important fungal, bacterial and viral diseases with symptoms, causal organisms and control are described as follows:

Soft mildew or cobweb (*Dactylium dendroides*)

A fluffy, white, cobweb-like mould grows over the surface of the casing soil. Initially it is white but later changes to pink with age. This fungus attacks mushrooms which appear like white cottony balls on the surface but are totally rotten inside.

The chief sources of infection are soil, air, wet surface, high humidity and butts of mushrooms left in the cropping trays.

Control: Good ventilation and prevention of excess of humidity checks the disease. Individual patches are treated with 0.2 per cent dithane Z-78. They can also be covered with PCNB (penta chloro nitro benzene). In addition, the mushroom house must be disinfected with formalin before putting the trays in the room for the next season.

Brown plaster mould (*Papulospora byssina*)

It occurs on spawned and cropping trays. First it is white with a cloudy appearance, later the colour changes to brown. This fungus spreads very fast and causes heavy reduction in yield. Originally the fungus is present in the compost. Too wet compost, high temperature (28 to 32°C) during spawn run and cropping at more than 18°C encourages infection.

Control: Properly prepared compost, proper watering, maintaining suitable temperature during the spawn run and cropping, and 2 per cent formalin spray can also control the disease.

White plaster mould (*Scopulariopsis fumicola*)

It closely resembles brown plaster mould intially but later on from white it changes to a delicate pink shade. If compost making is improper then this fungus covers the whole tray and thus reduces the yield. Too much water in the compost during composting or an anaerobic peak heat are the main contributory factors for the growth of this fungus. Inoculum is carried by pests or air.

Olive green mould (*Chaetomium olivacearum*)

This fungus appears in the compost or spawned bed before casing. Initially it is white but afterwards changes to an olive green colour.

Improper pasteurisation of the compost, inadequate ventilation and too wet compost are the source of this disease.

Control: Sufficient air should be introduced without increasing the temperature above 60°C during pasteurisation. Spraying of trays with 0.2 per cent thiram and captan or 0.05 per cent benlate can check the spread.

Inky cap (*Coprinus lagopus* and *C. comatus*)

The disease can be detected by the appearance of a long slender stalk with a small thin cap which is auto-deliquescent and dissolves into black inky liquid. The appearance of the fungus shows the presence of ammonia in the compost.

Control: Before filling the trays the compost should be free from ammonia, otherwise *Coprinus* spp. will appear and cease the yield of *Agaricus bisporus.* If the fruiting of *Coprinus* bodies is profuse in the spawned trays then the compost should be re-pasteurised at 60°C for two hours and then respawned and recased.

Green mould (*Trichoderma viride*)

It appears as green patches on the spawned and cased trays. If this fungus attacks the spawned tray the spawn run is affected. If it appears on the casing soil it checks the pin formation of the mushroom. This fungus grows on decomposed organic matter and dead mushroom tissues. Improper pasteurisation of compost and high humidity are also responsible for the spread of this fungus. The spores of this fungus are carried away by air, water and careless handling.

Control: Spraying with 0.05 per cent benlate checks the disease.

Truffle disease (*Pseudobalsamia microspora*)

This disease is more prevalent in summer. The fruiting body of this fungus appears in mushroom beds as a round, cream coloured, wrinkled and convoluted surface, giving it a brain-like appearance, having characteristic small form in the bed and top of casing soil (resembling fused pinheads). These bodies on maturity turn reddish brown and release the spores. Lack of ventilation and high humidity are the main factors for the appearance of this disease. The only control measure is that spawn run temperature and the cropping bed temperature should not exceed 18°C with adequate ventilation. High humidity in the mushroom house should also be avoided to control the truffle fungus.

Bubble disease (*Mycogone perniciosa*)

When this fungus attacks the mushroom, it covers the mushroom with a dense white mat of mycelium leading to reduction in yield. In the early stage of its infection the mushroom has a swollen stalk and a disproportionately small cap. The casing soil may be the source of infection, but other agencies also can not be overlooked as the sources of infection such as unpasteurised compost, high humidity, etc. Temperature above 17°C are favourable for the development of the disease.

Control: The diseased mushroom should be sterilised on the beds with 2 per cent formalin and should be promptly removed. The infected area may also be sprayed with 0.2 per cent dithane Z-78, and benlate 0.05 per cent. Benlate may be mixed in casing soil also.

Dry bubble, brown spot disease (*Verticillium malthousei* or *V. psiallistae*)

This fungus causes light brown spots on the cap which coalesce and cover most of the area of the cap resulting in irregular patches. In severe infection the mushroom becomes distorted. The cap shrinks and the affected mushroom becomes leathery. The primary source of infection is the casing soil. Control of high temperature during cropping and proper ventilation is advisable for the control of the disease, 0.2 per cent dithane Z-78 spraying three times, at the time of casing, pin head formation and after two flushes of the crop, is effective.

Bacterial blotch (*Pseudomonas tolaassi*)

This bacterial disease causes brown, slightly sunken blotches on the mushroom cap. These spots are irregular, yellowish to dark brown and coalesce in the later stage (Fig. 6.10).

The main source of infection is the casing soil. Infection spreads through water, flies, mites, nematodes, etc. The casing soil should

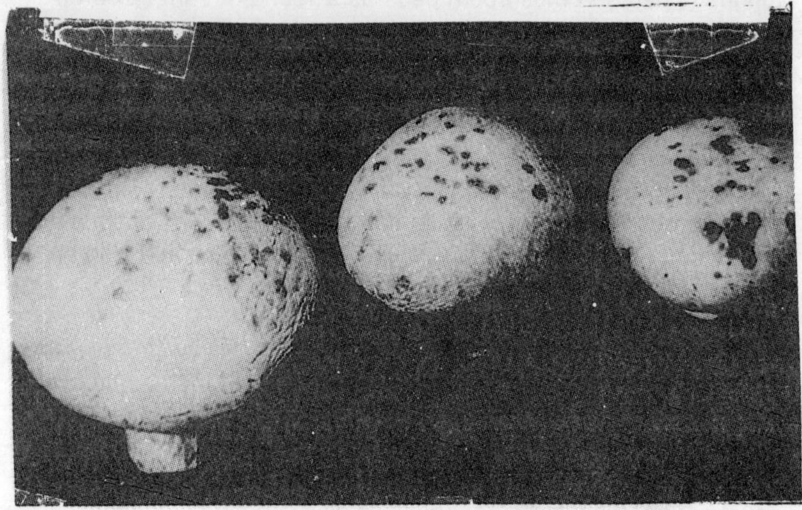

Fig. 6.10. Bacterial Blotch Disease.

be properly sterilised and ventilation should be quite adequate. Use of chlorinated water also reduces the disease incidence. Before the pin formation, preventive spray with 9 mg/ft of terramycin on the beds is advisable. Spraying in between the flushes is also quite effective if the disease persists.

Virus diseases

None of the virus diseases is reported from India but there are reports from other countries. Various names like La France (Sinden and Hauser, 1950), Brown disease and watery stipe, (Gandy, 1960), X disease, (Kneebone *et al.,* 1962), and dieback disease (Gandy and Hollings, 1962) were given according to the symptoms observed. Under dry conditions diseased mushrooms are shrivelled, leathery and brown in colour. Under humid conditions the stipe becomes watery and grey. Sometimes an abnormal elongation of the stipe with tilted pileus (drum stick) are noticed. Delayed appearance of pin heads, and early maturity of sporophore are also the symptoms of the virus disease. Virus infection may even be symptomless (Nair, 1972). It has been observed that the cream and off-white variety of mushrooms usually suffer less damage than the pure white variety.

Six viruses have been isolated from the diseased mushrooms. Five of them are polyhedral having particles 19, 25, 29, 35 and 50 nm in diameter, and one is bacilliform particle 19 × 50 nm (Hollings and Stone, 1969, 1971; Nair, 1972). They can occur singly or in combinations. It is difficult to associate any particular type of virus with any specific symptom. Transmission of virus through phorid larvae and Tarsonemus mites are reported by Hussay (1972). Transmission through mushroom spores (Schisler *et al.,* 1967) and through mushroom spawn are reported by Nair (1972). Certain species of field mushroom, e.g., *Laccaria laccata* have been suspected as natural reservoirs of mushroom viruses.

Control

Zaayen (1972) suggested the following control measures:

1) Heat the growing room, along with trays and compost at 70°C for 12 hours at the end of the crop.

2) Treat the trays and other equipment with 4 per cent sodium pentachlorophenate, 0.5–1 per cent soda (Na_2CO_3) solution.

3) Disinfect the doors, floor, and walls etc., with 4 per cent formaldehyde solution. Strict hygiene should be observed at the mushroom farm to eliminate the virus disease to some extent.

Insect pests

Mushrooms are also attacked by insect pests. It is better to prevent the entry of these. Once mushrooms are infested with insects it is difficult to control them. Spring tails, phorids flies, sciarid flies, mites and nematodes and small larvae of mushroom flies bore the fruiting bodies and cause rotting. Some pests cause damage to the spawn and hence lead to reduction in yield. They lay eggs and the larvae feed on the compost, eat away the mycelium and burrow into the stalk of the mushroom. The mature larvae are easily recognised by their black head and elongated shape.

Sciarids

These flies are dark in colour and have slender bodies with long antennae. Flies themselves cause little harm to the mushroom bed, but its larvae are more harmful. These flies lay eggs in the bed and the larvae that hatch out, feed on the compost and burrow into the base of the stalk right through to the cap. Sometimes the flies lay eggs on the cap and the larvae tunnel down into the mushroom, making funnel-shaped cavities. Larvae are black in colour and 6 to 7 cm long and can be recogonised by their black head and elongated shape. Common are: *Lycorella fenestralis, Neosciara pauciseta, Sciara carpophilla, S. multiseta, S. agaria.*

Phorids

These have short antennae and wing venation. In early summer and late autumn much damage is done by the larvae of these insects which can be distinguished by the lack of a distinct black head. Their front end is tapered. Phorids cause much damage to the mycelium but sometimes they make tunnels into the mushroom. These flies are quite active during the early hours of day. The common varieties are: *Megaselia nigra, M. agrici, M. bovistra, M. flavinervis and M. halternata.*

Spring tails

These are quite tiny and cannot be seen with the naked eye. These have stout antennae. They can crawl with speed, but they move by springing several inches into the air. When they are in a mass they look like gun powder on beds. They mostly feed on the mycelium and may sometimes attack the stalks and caps also. Common among them are: *Lepidocyrtus cyaneus, L. lanuginosus, Achorutes armatus, Isotoma simplex, Prerstoma minuta, Xenylla* sp. (Bahl *et al.*, 1981).

Cecid

These are tiny orange black flies, which are seen rarely, but their presence is indicated by the appearance of very small larvae, which are smaller than those of phorids and sciarids. They are pinkish yellow, orange or white, pointed at both ends and very often have a dark "anchor" like structure in the neck. They eat the mycelium but mostly make their way into the stalk and gills. Common among them are: *Heteropeza xygmaea, Myophila spyeri, M. barnesi, Lestremia cinerea.*

Mites

These are found in the mushroom house. They do not cause damage to the mushroom but are the carrier of the inoculum. They eat the mycelium and also make holes in the mushroom caps and stalks, and sometimes they chew the mycelial strands around the bases of the stalks. *Rhizoglyphus, Phylloxerea, Tyrophagus lintneri, T. putrescentiae, T. longior, Histiostoma gracilipes, Pygmephorus americanus, Tarsonemus floricolus, Linopodes antennaepes* are commonly found.

Nematodes

The faulty method of compost making and casing soil are the main cause of the occurrence of nematodes. There are three types of nematodes found in the mushroom beds. The parasitic nematodes have a spike-like structure called stylet. The nematodes project the stylet, punctures the mycelium and sucks its contents. They puncture the mycelium at several points and thus the mycelium start disappearing. The compost becomes sodden. Nematodes also feed on the mushroom, turning them brown, watery and stunted. In this group belongs, *Ditylenchus mycelophagus* and *Aphelenchoides composticola, A. aesterocaudatus* (Bahl *et al.*, 1981).

The other category of nematodes possess a tubular mouth. They feed on bacteria in the compost by sucking liquid and organic matter. The nematode excretes waste material which are toxic to the mushroom mycelium and when the nematode population becomes too high the mycelium is killed due to high toxicity. In addition, the nematodes are also carriers of phathogenic bacteria (*Pseudomonas tolaassi*).

Control

1) Dust lindane (0.65 per cent) 80 g/quintal of straw to be mixed at the 7th turn during compost preparation.

Fungicides for Mushroom Diseases, Fletcher *et al.* (1986)

Common name	Trade name (and manufacturer)	Method and rate of use	Fungi controlled
Benomyl*	Benlate (Du Pont)	Mix with casing or apply in place of first watering Mix 240 g/100 m^2 (0.5 lb/1000 ft^2) Drench 240 g/200 litres/ 100 m^2 (0.5 lb/40 gall/1000 ft^2)	*Dactylium, Mycogone, Trichoderma, Verticillium*
Carbendazim*	Bavistin (BASF)	Mix with casing or apply in place of first watering. Mix 250 g/100 m^2 (8 fl oz/ 1000 ft^2) Drench 250 ml/200 litres/ 100 m^2 (8 fl oz/40 gal/1000 ft^2)	*Dactylium, Mycogone, Trichoderma, Verticillium*
	Bavistin Flowable (BASF)	Use as for Bavistin. Mix 250 ml/100 m^2 (8 fl oz/1000 ft^2 Drench 250 ml/200 litres/ 100 m^2 (8 fl oz/40 gal/1000 ft^2)	
Chlorothaloni	Bravo 500 (SDS Biotech)	Apply as a spray 1 week after casing and repeat if necessary not less than 2 weeks later	*Mycogone, Verticillium*
	Repulse (Midox)	Rate 220 ml in 100-200 litres/100 m^2 (7 fl oz/20-40 gal/100 yd^2)	
Prochloraz manganese	Sporgon (FBC)	Used as either a single, double or triple application. Single: 7-9 days after casing, 300 g/100 litre/100 m^2 (10 oz/20-25 gal/1000 ft^2) Double : 7-9 days after casing and between second and third flushes, 113 g/100 litre/100 m^2 (4 oz/20-25 gal/1000 ft^2) Triple : 7-9 days after casing and after first and third flushes, 57 g/100 litres/100 m^2 (2 oz/20-25 gal/1000 ft^2)	*Dactylium, Mycogone Verticillium*
Thiabenzazole*	Hymush (Agrichem Ltd)	Mix into casing or apply as spray. Mix 180-250 g (6.5-8.5 oz)/200 litre (45 gal) When disease is serious, supplement above with 90g (3 oz)/100 m^2/200 litre between	*Dactylium, Mycogone, Verticillium*

Common name	Trade name (and manufacturer)	Method and rate of use	Fungi controlled
		flushes or: No initial treatment but weekly applications of 150 g (4 oz)/200 litres/100 m*) *NB*: Maximum amount to be used is 750 g 24 oz)/100 m^2 to any one crop. A single initial dose should not exceed 250 g (8 oz) and supplementary does 120 g (4 oz)/100 m^2.	
	Tecto Flowable (Merck, Sharp & Dohme)	Used as for Hymush	*Mycogone, Verticillium*
Zineb	Zineb 7% Dust (Hortag)	Occasional treatment after casing and between breaks. Rate, 250 g/100 m^2 (12 oz/1000 ft^2) or, applied every week after casing throughout cropping and before watering 140 g/100 m^2 (4.5 oz/1000 ft^2)	*Dactylium, Mycogone, Red geotrichum, Verticillium*
	Zineb Wettable (Hortag)	After casing and between flushes, 1 kg/1000 litres at rate of 5 litres/10 m^2 (1 lb/100 gal at rate of 1 gal/100 ft^2)	*Dactylium, Mycogone*
	Tritoftorol (Bos Chemicals)	Between flushes, 5 kg/100 m^2 at 4.5 litres/4.6 m^2 (0.5 lb/100 gal at 1 gal/50 ft^2)	*Dactylium, Mycogone*

* Benzimidazole fungicides

Insecticides for Mushroom Pests (Fletcher *et al.* 1986)

Common name	Trade name	Method and rate of use	Organisms controlled
Diazinon (Ciba-Geigy)		Mix with compost at spawning	
	Basudin 5G	200 g/tonne (7 oz/ton)	
	Basudin 40 WP	25 g/tonne (1 oz/ton)	Phorids*
	Diazitol liquid	56 ml/tonne (2 fl oz/ton)	
	Basudin 5G	1 kg/tonne (36 oz/ton)	
	Basudin 40 WP	125 g/tonne (4.5 oz/ton)	Sciarids*† and
	Diazitol liquid	278 ml/tonne (10 ft oz)/ton) If incorporated before peak-heat, double the above rates must be used	decids*
Dischlorvos (Ciba-Geigy)	Darmycel	Aerial spray in spawn-running rooms	

Common name	Trade name	Method and rate of use	Organisms controlled
	dichlorvos	30 ml in 300 ml water /140 m³ (1 fl oz in 0.5 pint water/5000 ft³)	Phorids and sciarids†
Diflubenzuron (IC-Midox)	Dimilin	Mix with casing 120 g/tonne (4.5 oz/ton)	Sciarids
	Dimilin	Drench top cassing**) 4 g in 2.5 litres water/m² (13.5 oz in 50 gal water/1000 m²)	Sciarids
Chlorfenvinphos (Ciba Geigy)	Sapecron 24 EC Sapecron 10G	Mix with compost at spawning 208 ml/tonne (7.5 oz/ton) 500 g/tonne (18 oz/ton)	Sciarids*† and phorids
	Sapecron 24 EC Sapecron 10G	Mix with casing 125 ml/tonne (4.5 oz/ton) 300 g/tonne (10.75 oz/ton)	Sciarids*†
Malathion (Murphy)	Malathion 60	Drench to casing 330 ml in 200 1 water/100 m² (II fl oz in 40 gal water/1000 ft²)	Sciarids†
Gamma-HCH (Octavius-Hunt)	Fumite lindane pellets	Aerial smoke during cropping Pellet size 3, treats 84 m³ (3000 ft³)	Phorids and sciarids
Resmethrin/ pyrethrins (Mitchell-Cotts)	Pynosect 30	Aerial spray during cropping 30 ml/100 m² (1 fl oz/1000 ft²)	Phorids and sciarids
Resmethrin (PBI)	Turbair resmethrin extra	Aerial spray during cropping 30 ml/100 m² (1 fl oz/1000 ft²)	Phorids and sciarids
Permethrin (ICI-Midox)	Ambushfog 2	Aerial application during cropping 100 ml/250 m³ (4.5 fl oz/10 000 ft³)	
(PBI)	Turbair permethrin	30 ml/100 m³ (1 fl oz/1000 ft²)	Phorids and sciarids
(Octavius-Hunt)	Fumite permethrin smokes	Canistre size 4000, treats 112 m³ (4000 ft³)	
Pirimiphos-methyl (ICI-Midox)	Actellifog	Aerial fog during cropping 70 ml/100 m² (2.25 fl oz/1000 ft²)	Phorids and sciarids

* Manufacturer's label recommendations differ from those quoted above

** These figures are based on a prepared casing weight of 1 tonne/30 m² (3 tons/ 1000 ft²)

† Sciarid populations that are resistant to organophosphorous insecticides will not be controlled with these chemicals.

2) Spraying the spawned trays with 7 ml melathion (50 per cent E.C.) in 10 litres of water 2 days after spawning and 2 days before casing.

3) Add 40 ml of nemagon in 10 litres of water at the time of the second turn per 300 kg of wheat straw compost for nematodes.

4) Spray the trays with 5 ml of nuvan (100 of E.C.) in 10 litres of water during spawn run and 2 ml in 10 litres of water during cropping.

5) Cultural practices.

Abnormalities of mushrooms

Rose comb

In this case the cap is malformed and gills or lamella formed on its upper surface. On top of the cap of the mushroom appears a pink, waft-like outgrowth composed of a mass of irregular and ill-formed gills. The abnormality is caused by the use of mineral oils or their fumes in the mushroom house. Spraying of water without cleaning the spraying machine used for diesel oil or other mineral oil, use of oily water, frequent pesticidal spraying, use of coal or kerosene oil stove to heat the mushroom house are the causes of this. All the foregoing things should be avoided in the mushroom house. If one is using sawdust, or a kerosene oil stove for heating purposes one should be particular that the fumes of the oil gas should not circulate in the mushroom house.

Long stalked mushroom

Improper ventilation in the mushroom production room leads to the formation of long stalk and small cap (Fig. 6.11).

Scaly and cracked mushroom

This deformity is due to draught or cold air or less humidity in the production room (Fig. 6.12).

Open mushrooms

Due to the high temperature of the production room, premature opening of the caps occur. This opening may be due to high concentration of carbon dioxide also.

Stroma

White mycelial growth on the casing soil which makes a compact structure of the mycelium hinders the pin formation of the

Fig. 6.11. Long Stalked Mushroom.

mushroom. This is also due to less humidity and high concentration of carbon dioxide. It is advisable to re-case the trays.

Preservation

Mushrooms, like fruits and vegetables, are highly perishable. They grow in flushes and every 8 to 10 days they are harvested in abundance. In between the flushes the production comes down quite low. The demand never coincides with the supply, the day when there is good production the demand may be low and *vice versa*. To prevent such a glut in the fresh market, it is necessary to preserve them. Mushrooms require a great deal of attention during storage, marketing and processing at the post harvest stage. Discolouration, weight and flavour loss are some of the problems.

Garmley and Mac Canna (1967) reported that the mushrooms covered with a synthetic PVC film lose water and whiteness at a much slower rate than uncovered mushrooms. They suspected that the change in colour is due to loss in moisture. Mushrooms stored at 21°C remained whiter than those stored at 1°C or 11°C, but they mature at a much faster rate. The loss of whiteness during storage is a complex process. They found that the mushrooms stored at 21°C hardened at a faster rate than mushrooms stored at 11°C or 1°C. According to them, the chemical action plays a great role in the toughening process. Mushrooms stored at 21°C (RH 74-85) did not lose whiteness as quickly as those stored at 11°C (RH 50-60) or 1°C (RH 70-80). Toughening and the degree of maturity were greatest at 21°C. Different methods are given here to increase the shelf life of white button mushrooms.

Storage in fresh conditions

Mushrooms have a high rate of respiration and hence proper attention should be given during storage. In Western countries white button mushrooms are covered with PVC film and have a shelf-life of 5 to 7 days at 15 to 21°C temperature during transportation. Uncovered mushrooms have 2 to 4 days of shelf-life under similar conditions.

Mushrooms packed in fibre board trays (1.5 m × 1.5 m × 4 cm) covered with an inverted tray to reduce desiccation show a maximum shelf-life of 7 days when kept at 1°C for 5 days and 20°C for the next 2 days (Bano and Patwardhan, 1979).

Vacuum cooling also helps in increasing the shelf-life. In this case mushrooms are packed in a film which is punctured to allow evaporation from the mushrooms. The punctured hole is covered with a small piece of sticking tape after vacuum cooling to stop the gas flow and to allow the overwrap to function properly.

Fresh mushrooms are packed in 0.02 to 0.03 mm dense polyethylene bags with nitrogen and can be stored well at 0°C up to 5 weeks, at 5°C up to 4 weeks and at 15°C up to 2 weeks.

In South India fresh mushrooms are sent to other places by packing in polythene bags and these are kept in paper lined bamboo baskets or in corrugated cardboard.

Controlled atmosphere

Shelf life of fresh mushrooms is increased in a controlled atmosphere consisting of 9 per cent oxygen and 25 per cent carbon dioxide. Partial evacuation followed by flushing with carbon monoxide and storage at low temperature can also extend the storage-life up to 20 days.

Preservation by gamma radiation

Shelf life of mushroom can be increased up to 10 days by giving gamma radiation of 250 Krad dose and storing mushroom at 15°C (Roy and Bahl, 1984)

Freeze drying

It is done by immersing the sliced mushroom in a solution of 0.05 per cent sodium metabisulphate and 2 per cent salt for about 30 minutes. These are then blanched in boiling water for 2 minutes, followed by cooling. The product is frozen at -- 22°F for one minute. The frozen mushrooms are dried to a moisture content of 3 per cent in a freeze drier and packed in cans under vacuum. In the second method after harvesting the mushrooms are pre-cooled to temperatures of 2 to 4°C. At the freezing plant they are sorted out, washed, and pre-treated. Chlorine levels as high as 50 ppm have been helpful in keeping the microbial load to a minimum since the frozen mushrooms are sold to reprocessors.

Some people blanch the mushrooms as is done for canning, and then keep it in deep freeze as it will retain its white colour for a longer period.

Steeping preservation (Dang and Singh, 1978)

Edible mushrooms have been steeped in a solution of 2.5 per cent salt, 0.1 per cent ascorbic acid, 0.2 per cent critic acid, 0.1 per cent sodium bicarbonate and 0.1 per cent potassium metabisulphite to give organoleptically acceptable mushrooms with no microbial spoilage up to 10 days in storage.

Dehydration of mushrooms

For dehydration purposes mushrooms are harvested at a mature stage. If the stalk is too big it is cut into small pieces. Mushrooms can be dried in the sun or in a mechanical dehydrator at 60 to 70°C. After complete drying the mushrooms are reduced to nearly one-tenth of their weight. Dried mushrooms should be stored in air-tight containers in a cool dry place. Dried mushrooms can also be ground into powder which can be used for making mushroom soup. The powder should be packed in an airtight container.

Mushrooms can also be dried after steam or water blanching and drying at 60 to 70°C. Dipping in aqueous solution of chlorine, following sulphiting is reported to give whiteness to the product. Dried mushrooms are hermetically sealed so that they retain their original colour and flavour for six to seven months during storage. These are better reconstituted by immersing in an aqueous solution of sugar and ascorbic acid.

Canning of mushroom (Sethi and Anand, 1978)

Button mushrooms can be canned either whole, sliced or in smaller pieces. Canners prefer mushrooms to be picked at an early stage. Immediately before canning, the stalks are cut close to the button and the mushrooms showing any blemishes are rejected. Mushrooms used for canning purposes should be small buttons and of the same size, with 0.4 to 1.0 cm long stalk attached to the cap. Later, mushrooms are washed gently to remove any adhering soil. Blanching is necessary to control discolouration but this causes shrinkage. Shrinkage up to 30 to 35 per cent may be allowed. Rough handling of blanched mushrooms also causes increase in the shrinkage percentage. Fresh mushrooms are dipped in boiling water for 2 to 3 minutes and put in cold water to prevent leaching losses which are sometimes as high as 25 per cent or by immersing mushrooms in a boiling solution of 0.1 to 0.2 per cent citric acid for about 5 minutes (Dang and Singh, 1978) and cooled immediately in cold water.

Blanched and cooled mushrooms are filled in cans leaving 1.25 cm space. Approximately 195 g mushrooms are filled in 1 lb jam cans. Brine solution consisting of 2 per cent common salt, 2 per cent sugar and 0.3 per cent citric acid is boiled, filtered through muslin cloth and added into the can to fill just up to the brim (125 ml solution for 1 lb jam can). After placing the lid on the can the mushrooms are exhausted by keeping them in boiling water till the centre temperature reaches 80 to 85°C. After placing the lids they are sealed on a seamer to get an airtight seam. The 1 lb cans are later steamed at 115°C (10 lb/p. si) for 25 to 30 minutes. This time should be increased or decreased depending on the larger or smaller size of the can. Soon after sterilisation, the cans are kept in fresh water for cooling. Later, they are wiped dry and kept in a cool dry place.

According to Dang and Singh (1978), canning of mushrooms can be improved if the fresh mushrooms are exposed to vacuum treatment by immersing in plain water or in a 2 per cent brine solution in a vacuum even before blanching. Before evacuation or breaking of vacuum, it is essential to press the floating mushroom below water level to achieve desired results. Grading practices can be employed by physical means to give a better look to the product. The main problem in the canning of mushroom is its browning. In Europe, to improve the colour of the product, blanching of mushrooms is often done in a citric acid solution. Ascorbic acid and EDTA (Ethylene Diamine Tetra Acetic) acid in the ratio of 1 : 10 is also sometimes used in covering brine. Immersing in sulphite solution of sulphur prior to blanching has also reported to improve the colour of the product.

An increase of 19 per cent in the weight of the canned product has been reported when the fresh mushrooms were stored for 72 hours at 12°C and 95 per cent RH. The increased weight was attributed to the greater water holding capacity of mushrooms that develops during storage. It was observed that an interaction existed between soaking and cold storage which was effective in increasing the yield of canned mushrooms.

Mushrooms are also preserved in the form of pickles and ketchup.

Do's and Don'ts of Mushroom Growing

1) Take full precautions while making the compost. There should not be any ammonia smell when the compost is ready.

2) The compost should not be too wet or too dry at the time of filling. If it is dry, then sprinkle water over the compost before filling the boxes.

3) The success of mushroom growing depends on the compost.

4) Boxes should be filled up to the brim with the compost.

5) Spawn should be from a reliable source.

6) Do not use contaminated spawn.

7) After spawning cover the boxes with newspaper. Watering should be avoided during the spawn run. If watering is essential,

spray water over the newspaper with a fine jet.

8) The casing soil should be properly sterilised. Don't sterilise the casing soil long before the use and store it for a longer period.

9) Casing soil should not be very fine otherwise there will not be a good gaseous exchange.

10) Before putting the casing over the spawn run compost, moisten it with water.

11) Cowdung used for the casing should be rotten and should be one year old.

12) Maintain the temperature of the room for 2 or 3 days at 22 to 24°C after casing and then lower the temperature to 14 to 18°C.

13) To keep the room humid and the temperature low, spray the walls and floor of the mushroom house with water.

14) If the weather is dry, hang moist gunny bags on the side of the trays and keep it moist or fill the gunny bags with saw dust and spray water over it to create humidity in the room.

15) If there is panning of the casing soil, rake the casing soil gently with a fork or with a pointed knife to provide the gas exchange.

16) If after raking there is no pinning, it is better to remove the whole casing soil and recase the bed.

17) If there is an appearance of disease in the box, treat the box immediately. If it does not respond to the treatment, remove the diseased tray immediately from the room.

18) Spray water gently, do not water the tray before picking.

19) After picking fill up the holes with sterilised casing soil and spray water.

20) For picking, if the mushroom is cut from the base then remove the remaining portion with the pointed knife. Don't leave it as such, otherwise other saprophytes and bacteria will attack it and will be the source of disease.

21) Keep the butts in one container and burn it or throw it in the pit far away from the mushroom house.

22) Never broom the mushroom house, dust and spores of micro-organisms will spread and will spoil the mushroom. Remove the dust by sweeping it gently with a duster.

23) Before entering the mushroom house, remove your shoes and put on the slippers kept separately in the mushroom house.

Mushroom Farm Design

Earlier mushroom growing was done in hilly areas, but now with the advancement of technology it can be done at all elevation/places in

India under controlled conditions with the specialised construction of mushroom houses.

In building a mushroom farm, there are number of initial considerations and in the fifties on that basis a standard plan was made, though with the advancement, the materials have been changed but the standard plans still remain the same.

Mushroom growing is an agricultural activity where the hygiene is the most important factor. In order to have reasonable income from mushroom farming, it should have at least six rooms, each with a cropping area of 200m^2. While setting a mushroom farm one should take further expansion into account.

After selection of the site the building should be planned, it should be near the wide road for delivery of raw material, dispatch of mushroom and spent compost. It is important that the plot is serviced for water, sewage, electricity and possible also natural gas.

For farm designing care should be taken that in small piece of land different operations such as composting, spawn making, cropping and post-harvest technology should be done in most efficient way at low cost.

For Button mushroom the infrastructure needed are (Fig. 6.17)

1. Covered composting yard with guddy pit,
2. Bulk/pasteurization chamber,
3. Cropping rooms,
4. Cold room,
5. Casing soil pasteurization room,
6. One boiler room,
7. A/C handling room,
8. Store

The foundation of the building should be on the firm ground. Water pipes, electrical cables and sewers are laid before the actual construction starts. The site should be away from the populated area. The composting yard is built nearer to the main road for operation convenience. The bulk chambers are built on the order side of the composting yard so that the distant end of the chamber opens nearer to the cropping rooms. The cropping rooms are built away from composting area for maintaining the cleanliness. The casing pasteurization chamber is also built away from composting yard on one side of the bulk chambers. Space for future expansion should be left at the beginning of planned mushroom farm. In short :

1. Composting yard should be accessible by road and away from cropping rooms.

2. Preferably, the bulk chamber should be in line and close to the compsting yard.

3. Service rooms and machinery rooms have to be nearer to cropping rooms for greater efficiency.

4. Cropping rooms should be at the back of bulk chambers away from composting yard.

5. Extra space should be left for expansion of bulk chamber, compositing yard and cropping rooms.

6. Unit should be built where there is ample supply of water and power.

7. It should be preferably located outside the municipal limits.

To start with, one should have six growing rooms of 35' × 25' × 12', each room will have 20 tonnes of fresh compost. The size of the bulk chamber should match the capacity of the growing rooms. It is convenient and economical to have a bulk chamber of minimum 20 tonnes. Dimension of the bulk chamber should be 36' × 9' × 12' giving 20 tonnes of compost at a time: A composting yard 60' × 40' should also be constructed for preparation of compost. Such unit will yield between 90–100 tonnes of mushroom annually, if run on full capacity. One casing soil pasteurization room, one boiler room, one AC handling room and one store is also needed. The above bulk chamber should be 20–25m long, 10m wide with a height of about 4–4.5m, properly covered with iron galvanised iron sheet. Dtuch mushroom farm design is widely used all over the world. There are two systems of growing, single-zone system and dobule zone system. In single-zone system all the operation, i.e., peak heating, spawn running and cropping is done in a single room. Double-zone system, the compost after phase I is filled into specially built chamber which is appropriately insulated and provided with steam connection and air blowing system. Rest of the operations are done in specially insulated separate rooms.

For commercially viable unit, total infrastructure required.

Facility	Units	Size	Total area (Sq.ft.)
Cropping rooms	12	35' × 25' × 12'	10500
Corridor in the growing rooms			1125
Office (Production facility)	1	12' × 12' × 12'	360
A/C handling room	1	55' × 15' × 12'	225
Composting yard	1	70' × 40' × 20'	2400
Pasteuization tunnel	2	36' × 9' × 12'	648
Boiler/Generator room	1	20' × 12' × 12'	240
Casing soil pasteurization	1	15' × 12' × 12'	180
Mushroom Packing area	1	15' × 12' × 12'	180
Spawning area/room	1	20' × 15' × 12'	240
Total area			1600 (sq.ft.)

In addition to above, land would be required for casing soil dump, wheat straw and poultry manure storage and road paths, etc. Appropriate land required would be around 3500 sq.mts.

Construction and Insulation

Composting yard: Compost making by long and phase I of short method requires a covered shed without walls. The high roof and absence of walls will facilitate the escape of foul gas into the atmosphere. The composting yard should be laid on a firm ground. Bed of sand 15–20 cm thick is first laid, followed by a layer of concrete (15 cm thick). The floor must be well laid out and also allow smooth operation of door of bulk chamber. The floor is given a run off 1 cm per running meter away from the bulk chamber towards the guddy pit. The guddy pit should be 2 × 2 × 3m in dimension with a dewatering pump and a hose for spyaying back the run off water on the compostiong material. The roof of the outdoor composting platform is built on tresses or RCC pillars 15' high with a GI roofing.

The composting yard should be big enough to hold compost stack for phase I of composting and the size of the composting yard will be determined by the number and the capacity of bulk chambers. On an average, one tonne compost occupies about one metre length of the compost yard with extra space of 5m on each side for turning the composting material. A drain should run on two sides of platform away from the wall to facilitate periodic cleaning of platform.

Peak heating chamber/bulk chamber/tunnel

Bulk chambers/tunnel is required for mass treatment of the compost. Location of the tunnel in the mushroom growing unit is very important. The following parameters will influence its location:

a. The risk of infection
b. Location relative to the growing rooms
c. The ease of connection to the site services
d. Transporting of compost
e. The possibility of expansion

After phase I the compost is shifted to peak heating chamber/ bulk chamber/tunnel for pasteurization. For this, an insulated chamber is built with the facility for steam inlet, blower and controlled fresh air entry. The purpose is cutting off the external environment and creating the controlled fermentation of composting ingredients. Two types of chambers are used. For single zone system where all the operations are done in one room, the rooms are very well insulated and provided with steam, air handling cooling and heating facilties. This system proves efficient in already built structure like cold storages, where the entire space is utilized maximum without investing in construction of bulk chamber. The single zone system is labour economic but it is costly, because the capital cost is higher as all the rooms will be equipped with the facilities for all the operations to be carried out in series. In two zone system, compost is prepared in separate chamber and growing is done in separate chamber.

The dimension of the bulk chamber depends on the quantity of the compost to be filled. The thickness of the beds of compost can vary according to the density which depends upon straw contents, straw hardness, quality of animal by products, moisture contents and degree of phase I composting. During peak heating about 25% of compost is lost during spawn running. The tunnel, therefore must be filled with 30% more of compost.

The floor of the bulk chamber is prepared just like the floor of composting yard i.e., the floor is first laid with a sand 15-20 cm thick, then spread a layer of broken brick/stone (rori) 10 cm thick, followed by 5 cm concrete floor (1:2:6) and insulation with thermocol/glass wool 5 cm. thick (15kg/m^3 density) (Fig. 6.14). This will give K value of 0.5-0.6 K Cal/m^2 °C/hour. The insulation is covered with isolating membrane of PVC sheeting followed by 5 cm. concrete floor and finally the finish. The outer brick wall should be 22.5 cm thick over the concrete foundation floor and walls are separeted to leave space for expansion of construction under extremes of temperatue. This is done by filling 1 cm broad polystyrene battens to the base of the walls before pouring the concrete. They are burnt away later and the space is then filled with bituminous sealant.

The bulk rooms have double floor. The lower floor consists of an insulated concrete layer lying about half a meter below the level. The second floor consists of wooden beams or concrete grates with opening in between. All the openings should cover about 25% of the floor space. For good pressure distribution and free flow of air without any restriction, lower concrete floor is given 2% slope down to the air inlet. In a tunnel of 20 tonnes capacity, the plenum should be 3' deep at upper end. The floor must be laid with a good run off provided with a drain to facilitate the cleaning. Since, the temperature in the tunnel goes up to 60°C, its walls ceiling and the floor below the plenum should be well insulated.

The base of the tunnel (below grated floor) is full width ventilation duct. The blower, steam outlet from the boiler and re-circulation duct are provided on the deeper side of the tunnel. The plenum is divided with a perforated brick wall (one or two) in the centre for supporting the grated floor. The grating can be made of wood (painted with bituminous paint), coated iron strips mounted on angle iron frame or cemented, if possible. If nylon nets are to be used for mechanical filling and emptying, then cemented grated floor with appropriate RCC strength is built specially for the purpose. The doors of the bulk chamber are made of angle iron in wooden frame with 2-3" insulation in the middle and covered on both sides with aluminium sheets. Two vents are provided at the top of the tunnel, one connected to the blower through a recirculating duct and another provided for the exchange of surplus gases and water vapour from the tunnel. Fresh air in the tunnel is introduced via recirculating duct through dampers which are generally located at the top of the tunnel. This fresh air is filtered through 2μm filters. The tunnel should be hermetically sealed, insulated room without any leakage. A rubber gasket is provided on the inner side of the doors to make it leakproof. The chamber is serviced by a blower fan below the plenum, installed in underground room or on side of the chamber. The blower fan size will be in accordance with the tonnage of the compost in the bulk chamber.

A centrifugal blower fan, energized by a 7.5 HP motor with speed of 1440 rpm. will be able to produce necessary air pressure of 100-110mm of water level at entry point. The steam line is also connected at the entry point near the blower. The bulk chamber may have one door for filling and emptying the compost or two doors for filling and other for emptying the compost.

Roof is constructed just like that of the composting yard.

Initial Consideration/Work Plan

An air flow of 15–200 m³/per ton of compost is essential for effective well controlled pasteurization and optimum yields. Height of the compost in the tunnel is usually kept 2.0–2.2 metres and at this height 1 ton of compost needs floor area of about 1.1–1.2 m² or 900–1000 kg. compost per m² floor area can be filled in the tunnel. About 20–25% of the weight of compost is lost during pasteurization and 7–10% during spawn run i.e., about 1/3 of the original weight of compost is lost upto spawn run. One can say, if 10 qtls. of compost is loaded in the tunnel after phase 1 only 7.2–7.5 qtls will be available after phase II and about 6.8 qtls remain after spawn run. For 200 m² growing area with 90 kg of spawn run compost/m² then a total of 18 tonnes of spawn run compost or about 20 tonnes of un spawned compost is required or about 27 tonnes of fresh compost at filling. For this, one should start the composting with approximately 10 tonnes dry weight of the base material.

Compost should not be tightly filled in bulk chamber, it will result in poor aeration and low productivity.

Most of the air being circulated inside the tunnel, is the air exhausted in the space above the compost and blown inside under the ground floor through a blower. Only little fresh air is drawn inside through filter.

For bulk chamber to run most effectively necessary infrastructural construction has to be of exact specification. Any deviation from optimum standard will have detrimental effect on yield. Boiler and blower have to be of exact specification. For a standard tunnel of 20 tonnes capacity (ready to spawn compost), boiler of 300 lb/sq. inch should be good enough for effective pasteurization and conditioning. Blower fan of 1460rpm is required for effective circulation of air during processing, corresponding to air displacement of 200m^3, provided the grated floor is having 25–35% air gap.

Growing Rooms: The growing rooms should be according to the capacity of tunnel to accommodate the compost. For 20 tonnes of compost, room size should be 35' × 25' × 12' and growing rooms should be in line on both the sides. The foundation of growing rooms can be put like that of tunnel. The ground is generally not insulated. The walls of the growing room should be built of one brick having 3–5 cm thickness of insulating material inside, followed by cement plastering. Ceiling is made of 4" thickness RCC. The walls and the ceiling of the rooms must be damp proof. All joints in corrugated panels must be sealed from the above and the whole upper surface of the ceiling must be damp proof. Bituminous products are suitable. There are also other commercial products based on synthetic polymers. The damp proofing material must be applied sufficiently thick, to give a vapour barrier of at least 115μ thickness.

The damp proofing layer on the walls follows the same standard and either bitumen or white polymer paint may be used. In recent years white damp proofing paints have been used. Although they are expensive but gives pleasant working environment, better lighting, more hygiene. The surface must be smooth for better working.

The roof on the outside is protected by tarring it on top, followed by 10 cm thick loose soil, 5 cm thick mud capping and finally the tiles. This will protect the roof from weathering effects of rain and will ensure longer life of insulation and prevent seepage of moisture into the room in rainy season. In hilly areas with a high rain fall slanting GI sheet roof will be excellent and in that case mud capping and tiling of the roof is not done.

Single insulated door is made up of GI sheets or aluminium sheet. A rubber gasket is also provided in the door. Two vents (1.5"×15") provided in the opposite walls 2–3' above ground level. The vents are closed with wire nets and provided with insulated shutter for closing and opening. For change of air, a fresh air duct is provided on the top of the door made up of polythene sheets having small holes all over. This duct runs lenght wise in the room and is connected to the exhaust fan (24" diameter) energized by a 1.5 HP motor, mounted in a box, which is known as air handling equipment. This equipment has provision of cooling, heating and providing proper humidity in the rooms, and is installed in each growing room. The duct keeps the air movement within the room in permissible limit to prevent cracking of mushroom.

Ventilation System: Ventilation system can be: (a) under pressure system, (b) over pressure system. Under pressure system operating on 2 fans placed at two extractor openings, (40 × 40cm), present in the back wall. Two axial fans are fitted in these, each with capacity of 3000m^3/h giving a combined capacity of 4500 m^3/h in the cropping room after taking into consideration the resistance of spore filters at inlet openings. Single centrifugal fan for extraction can also be mounted in the opening above the door and in that case inlet openings are put at the sides and fitted with filters.

In overpressure system two outlet openings (40 cm × 40 cm) at the back of the room should be made with main inlet opening in front, with an axial fan and filter.

The distribution ducting must be carefully mounted in the centre of the room, while care must be taken to ensure even distribution by using a fixed duct with outlet holes/grills along its length. If an axial fan is used, rotation of the air must be stopped by using a distribution plate or honey comb.

On building of positive pressure with forced air circulation fan, the CO_2 laiden air will automatically be forced out of the back vents without allowing the entry of heat from outside to inside. When forced air circulation is not in use (during spawn run), the vents are to be closed with insulated panelled cover. During spawn run, the forced air circulation duct will work for cooling/heating of the air inside, with inner air recirculating in the room.

The important climatic factors in the growing room are; temperature, CO_2, relative humidity and air speed which have a direct bearing on crop yields.

The main emphasis has therefore, to be laid on providing the optimum conditions for various stages of growth in the cropping room i.e., vegetative growth and reproductive growth. For creating correct environmental conditions, the necessary infrastructure built has to be of the exact specification as mentioned above.

The growing rooms should have five shelves one above the other having wooden boards/GI sheets on all the four sides and bottom, keeping a distance of 60 cm each (Fig. 6.13). If cultivation is done in bags then four shelves can be installed, keeping minimum distance of 60–75 cm. each. Depth of compost in each bag should be 12–14", or in case of shelves 6–8". A room of standard size (35' × 25' × 12') can accommodate 3 rows of racks, each 5' wide. This will occupy 15' of the room land, the rest 10' can be used to have central paths of 3' each and two side paths of 2' each. Length of each rack would be 30'. In one growing room 20 tonnes of compost can be accommodated.

Seasonal Growing: Seasonal growing rooms are simple with some modifications. The growing rooms will have a cemented ceiling or a false ceiling with arrangement of forced air circulation (Fig. 6.15).

The forced air circulation is very essential in seasonal growing houses by installing an exhaust fan on top of the door fixing inwards; joined to a perforated polythene duct running along the entire length of the room. The walls and false ceiling should be air tight to make the forced air circulation system effective and work-

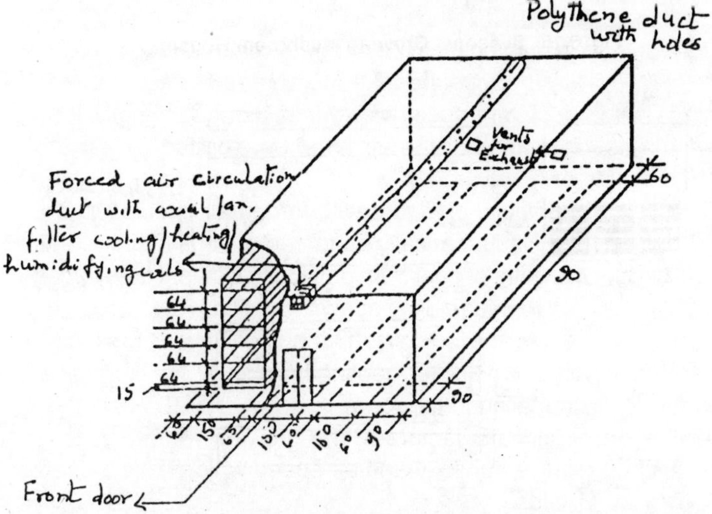

Fig. 6.13. View of Growing Rooms (Dimension in cm).

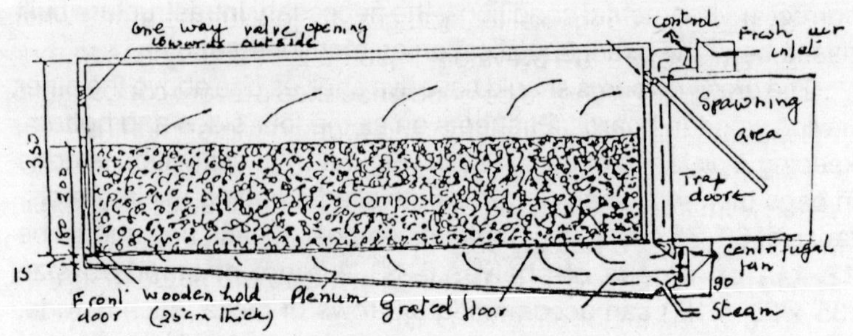

Fig. 6.14. Cross Section Bulk Chamber (Dimension in cm).

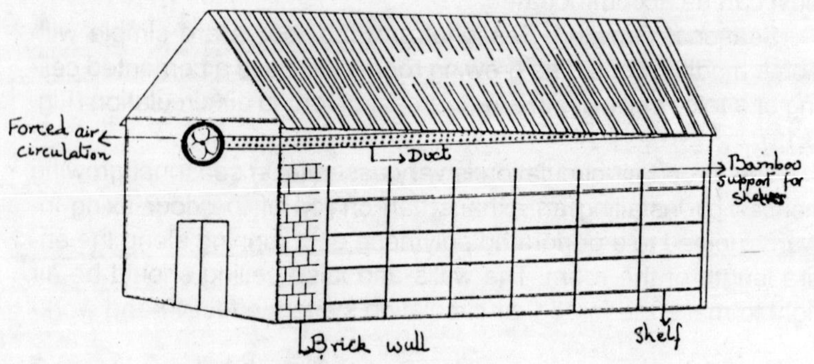

Fig. 6.15. Seasonal Growing Mushroom House.

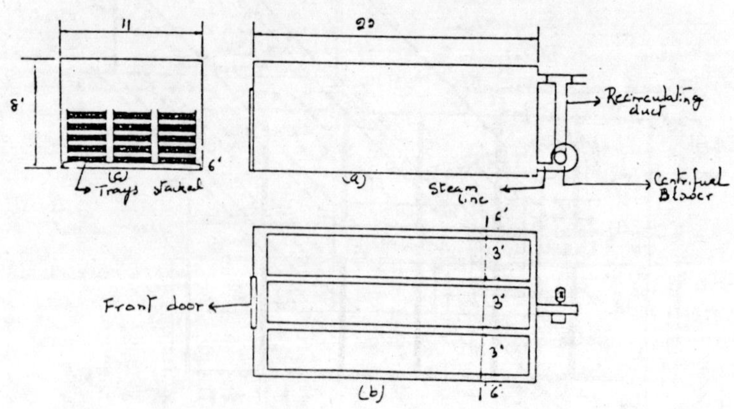

Fig. 6.16. Casing Pasteurization Chamber.

able. In low cost growing houses where thatched roof or asbestos sheets are used, false polythene ceiling will be good enough to create the sealing effect on top. The seasonal growing houses should not be insulated, as it will be difficult to maintain the environment inside the room congenial for crop growth. In extreme areas where lower temperature are prevalent in some part of the season, brick walls with air gaps should be good enough to prevent condensation of water on the walls in the cropping room in winter months.

Air changes, cooling/heating, RH, heat/CO_2 removal and evaporation from the beds is constantly maneuvered inside the cropping room for getting a healthy crop of mushrooms. All the above mentioned factors have to be maintained in the co-ordinated manner as change in one factor affects the other.

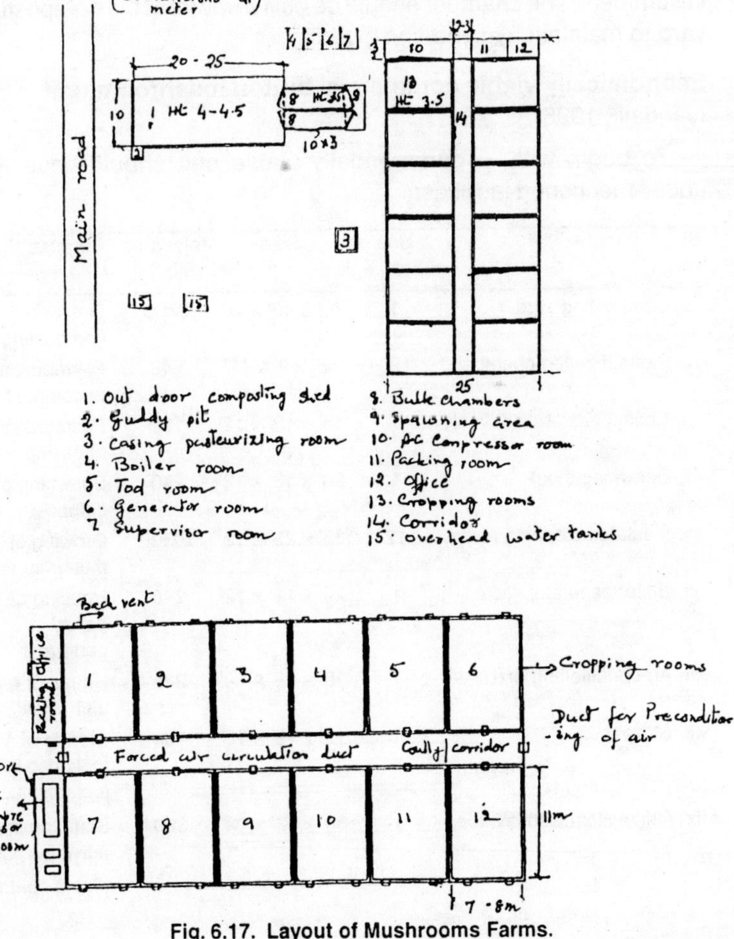

Fig. 6.17. Layout of Mushrooms Farms.

Casing pasteurization chamber

The casing pasteurizing chamber is an insulated chamber with a steam connection and a blower for effective circulation of steam inside the chamber, to achieve correct temperatures for pasteurization of the casing material. The size of the chamber depend upon the size of the compost chamber and the size of the growing rooms. One chamber load should provide casing for one compost lot from each tunnel. The casing after wetting is filled in the perforated wooden/aluminium trays which are placed one over the other inside the chamber. The door of the casing pasteurization chamber should also be insulated as in bulk chamber and made air-tight by fixing a rubber gasket on the inner boundary of the door. The casing chamber will also require the air handling equipment for cooling in summers. The chamber should be built away from the composting yard to maintain hygiene and cleanliness.

Economically viable commercial button mushroom unit
(Jandaik, 1995)

To begin with, a commercially viable unit should have the under-mentioned facilities:

Sl. No.	Facility	Unit	Size	Total area (sq.ft.)	Purpose
i.	Composting yard	1	70' × 40' × 20'	2800	Outdoor composting
ii.	Pasteurization chamber	2	36' × 9' × 12'	648	Pasteurization of compost
iii.	Casing pasteurization room	1	15' × 12' × 12'	180	Pasteurization of casing
iv.	Spawning room	1	20' × 12' × 12'	240	Spawning of compost
v.	Insulated cropping rooms	12	35' × 25' × 12'	10500	Growing of mushrooms
vi.	Boiler/generator room	1	20' × 12' × 12'	240	Housing of boiler/ generator
vii.	Air-conditioning unit	1	15' × 15' × 12'	225	House of A/C unit
viii.	Store room	1	15' × 12' × 12'	180	Storing of tools and implements, etc.
ix.	Office alongwith lavatory	1	30' × 12' × 12'	360	Staff/administrative purpose

(Table contd.)

x. Mushroom packing area	1	15' × 12' × 12'	180	Packing of mushrooms
xi. Water storage facility to be constructed over the roof	–	–	–	Supply of water
		15493 sq.ft or 16000 sq.ft		

Economics

Fixed costs

	Rs.
A. *Land procurement and development*	8,50,000.00
B. *Infrastructural facility*	
i) Construction of one composting yard at Rs. 125/– sq.ft	3,5,000.00
ii) Construction of pasteurization chamber including insulation at Rs. 275/– sq.ft	1,78,200.00
iii) Construction of pasteurization room at Rs. 200/– sq.ft	49,500.00
iv) Construction of one underground service room at Rs. 200/– sq.ft	25,600.00
v) Construction of spawning room/area	48,000.00
vi) Construction of boiler/generator and store rooms at Rs. 200/– sq.ft	84,000.00
vii) Costruction of over-head water tanks (25000 litres capacity)	50,000.00
viii) Construction of cropping rooms (12) including insulation charges at Rs. 275/– sq.ft	28,87,500.00
ix) Construction of A/C at Rs. 200/– sq.ft	45,000.00
x) Office/staff room and store room at Rs. 200/– sq.ft	72,000.00
xi) Mushroom packing room at Rs. 200/– sq.ft	36,000.00
	Total : Rs. 38,25,800.00
C. *Machinery*	
i) Central A/C facility consisting of one 100 tonnes capacity, compressor, chiller, condensor, air handing unit, etc.	25,00,000.00
ii) Boiler 300 kg evaporation/h capacity	2,50,000.00
iii) Generator 50 KVA capacity	4,00,000.00
iv) Understack blowers	30,000.00
v) Iron racks in the growing rooms and iron grating in the chamber	4,50,000.00
vi) Compost turner, mixer and filling line	1,75,000.00
vii) Electric and other installations	1,50,000.00
viii) Miscellaneous equipment like sprayers, buckets, forks, harvesting knives, trays, rubber pipes, weighing machine, etc.	1,00,000.00
	Total Rs. 40,55,000.00
Total cost (land + building + machinery)	Rs. 87,30,800.00

Variable Costs

A. *Raw marterials and other operational expenses*	
i) Wheat straw 400 tonnes at Rs. 1000 per tonne	4,00,000.00
ii) Chicken manure 225 tonnes at Rs. 350 tonne	78,750.00
iii) Casing soil procurement and its treatment (450 m³ at Rs. 100/m³)	45,000.00
iv) Spawn 18000 bags at Rs. 8 per bag	1,44,000.00

v) Gypsum, urea, pesticides/insecticides, etc.	50,000.00
vi) Electricity, fuel and water charges	3,00,000.00
vii) Miscellaneous expenses	12,000.00
viii) Risk factor at 4 per cent of the total raw material cost	41,190.00
	Total Rs. 10,70,940.00

B. *Manpower requirement and wages*

i) One Manager at Rs. 6,000 per month	72,000.00
ii) One Typist cum secretary at Rs. 3,500 per month	42,000.00
iii) One Jr. Engineer to look after the machinery at Rs. 4,500 per month	
iv) Total mandays involved in compost preparation and spawning, 40 mandays/outing. Total 50 outings in a year and wages involved at Rs. 30/– day	60,000.00
v) Labour requirement in the production unit at 70 man days/crop cycle/room i.e. 50 crop cycles at 100% capacity utilization (total 3500 man days at Rs. 30/– day)	1,05,000.00
	Total : 3,33,000.00

C. *Interest and Depreciation*

	Cost	Interest + Depreciation
		10,70,940.00
i) On buildings 2.5% depreciation and 12% interest	38,25,800.00	5,54,741.00
ii) On land (opportunity cost) 10% interest and no depreciation	8,50,000.00	85,000.00
iii) On machinery 10% depreciation and 12% interest	40,55,000.00	8,92,100.00
Total cost (i + ii + iii)		**15,31,841.00**

D. *Cost of Production and Return per Annum*

i) Raw materials	10,70,940.00
ii) Wages and salary	3,33,000.00
iii) Interest and depreciation	15,31,841.00
	Total 29,35,781.00
Total production at 100% capacity utilization at 18% conversion taking 4 crops of 90 days (15 days for spawning, 15 days for casing + 4 days for promordial initiation /development + 8 weeks picking) during each corp	144 tonnes of fresh mushrooms per year
Cost of production per kg fresh mushroom	20.31 or say Rs. 20
Income from sale of mushrooms at Rs. 30 per kg	43,20,000.00
Net profit per year.	13,84,219.00

Economics of Canned Product

i) Cost of A-10 can	Rs. 25.00
ii) Cost of canning and brine solution	Rs. 5.00
iii) Cost of mushroom 2 kg/drained weight, 3 kg fresh mushrooms at Rs. 25 per kg	Rs. 75.00
	Rs. 105.00
Sale price of one case containing 66 A-10 cans	$ 28.00/case (1$ = Rs. 32 or say Rs. 896/case
Total cans produced from 95 tonnes of mushrooms (95000 kg mushroom = 47500 cans)	7917 cases or 47500 cans
Sale price of 7917 cases at Rs. 896 per case	70,93,632.00
Cost of canning one A-10 can	105.00

Cost of one case of 6 cans	630.00
Total production cost of 7917 cases	49,87,710.00
Net profit	21,05,922.00

Economics of *agaricus bisporus* cultivation in northern plains with compost prepared by long method (based on information given by growers of Hisar/Sonepat) Jandaik, 1995.

	Rs.
A. *Fixed Costs*	
i) Land already available with the grower	
ii) Cost of construction of thatched house/mud house (25 × 6.3 M)	10,000.00
iii) Cost of racks made from bamboo and/or sticks	5,000.00
iv) Cost of spray pump, thermometer, forks, etc.	2,500.00
	Total : 17,500.00
B. *Variable Costs*	
i) Wheat straw 40 quintals at Rs. 100/– quintal	4,000.00
ii) Poultry manure 1000 kg at Rs. 12 per quintal	120.00
iii) Fertilizers	
a) Calcium ammonium nitrate 50 kg at Rs. 2 per kg	100.00
b) Urea 30 kg at Rs. 3 per kg	90.00
c) Superphosphate and potash (20 kg each) at Rs. 1.5 per kg)	60.00
iv) Molasses or wheat bran	350.00
v) Insecticide/fungicide, etc.	200.00
vi) Spawn 200 bottles (300 g in each bottle) at Rs. 8/– bottle	1,600.00
vii) Casing soil treatment charges	300.00
viii) Two labourers for 4 months at Rs. 30/– day	7,200.00
ix) 30 mandays for different turning of compost and fitting/spawing	900.00
x) Miscellaneous expenses	1,000.00
	Total : 15,920.00
C. *Depreciation and interest*	
Depreciation on A at 5% for kucha/mud structure and interest at 112% for 4 months	922.00
Total expenditure (B + C)	16,912.00
Anticipated yield at 10% conversion of compost	1200 kg
Cost of production per kg	14.00
Income from sale at Rs. 30/– kg.	36,000.00
Net income in 4 months	19,088.00

Economics of *white button* mushroom cultivation in hills with pasteurised compost (information given by a local grower at Solan)

	Rs.
A. *Fixed Costs*	
i) Land already available with the grower	
ii) Cost of construction of compost pasteurization tunnel (12 tonnes capacity)	55,000.00
iii) Cost of boiler (coal/diesel) and pipe fittings	60,000.00
iv) Blower and motor	18,000.00
v) (35' × 16' × 10') without insulation	1,10,000.00
vi) Cost of iron shelves (3 tiers)	40,000.00

vii) Cost of spray pump, forks, thermometer, etc.	2,000.00
	Total : 2,85,000.00

B. *Variable Costs*

i) Wheat straw 90 quintals at Rs. 100/q	9,000.00
ii) Poultry manure 45 quintals at Rs. 12/q	540.00
iii) Wheat bran 9 quintals at Rs. 320/q	2,880.00
iv) Urea 135 kg at Rs. 285/q	385.00
v) Gypsum 3 quintal	300.00
vi) Spawn 400 bags (purchased from University Spawn Lab.) at Rs. 8/- bag	3,200.00
vii) Polythene bags 55 kg. at Rs. 65/- kg.	3,575.00
viii) Labourers two for 4 months at Rs. 30/- day	7,200.00
ix) Additional labour (50 mandays) for turning of compost, filling and spawning	1,500.00
x) Fuel charges for pasteurization of compost and casing materials	3,000.00
xi) Electricity and water charges	1,800.00
xii) Insecticide, fungicide, etc.	2,000.00
xiii) Miscellaneous charges including marketing expenses	4,450.00
	Total : 40,740.00

C. *Depreciation and Interest*

Depreciation at 2.5% on building and 5% on machinery and interest at 12% on A	14,775.00
Total expenses (B + C)	55,515.00
Anticipated yield at 18% conversion of spawned compost	3,240 kg mushroom
Cost of production per kg. mushroom	Rs. 16.8 or say Rs. 17.00
Income from sale at Rs. 30/kg	97,200.00
Net profit in 4 months	41,685.00

Chapter 7

Cultivation of *Agaricus bitorquis*

Agaricus bitorquis is a new species and grows at a higher temperature and higher carbon dioxide concentration. It has a better shelf life as compared to *A. bisporus.* This mushroom is also knwon as the town or street mushroom in Europe. This species is resistant to die-back disease, so it can be a good replacement of *A. bisporus* in the areas where there is occurrence of die-back disease.

The fruit body of *A. bitorquis* is coarse with short stalk. The cap is silky white and sometimes a little indented.

These mushrooms are less inclined to become brown due to bruises and pressure. Some people like its "pronounced" taste and in later flushes the taste becomes stronger. The time between the formation of gills and the opening of veil is short. The difference with *A. bisporus* is that the first flush of *A. bitorquis* comes a little later and also the intervals between the flushes are more. The first flush generally appears between 22 to 26 days after casing and the second flush comes at the interval of 10 to 12 days. The compost which is used for the cultivation of *A. bisporus* can be used for the cultivation of *A. bitorquis.*

Spawning: The rate and method of spawning is the same as that of *A. bisporus.* The mycelium of *A. bitorquis* grows at a higher temperature. The average bed temperature during the mycelium growth should be about 30°C and the growing room should be ventilated as little as possible. Sometimes little ventilation is required to check the rising of bed temperature above 30°C. The mycelium of *Agaricus bitorquis* dies off after prolonged exposure to temperature above 34°C.

After 12 to 14 days of spawning the casing can be done. As the mycelium of *A. bitorquis* is finer, the compost at casing time will look less white than that of *A. bisporus.* A few weeks after casing the compost turns extremely white.

The same sterilised casing material as that of *A. bisporus* can be used for *A. bitorquis*. Reduction in depth of the casing layer, enhances the pin formation, but inversely affects the yield of the mushroom. A 4 cm casing layer gives better yield than 1.5 cm or 2 cm depth (Tewari and Sohi, 1978). In shallow layers, though the pin formation is earlier, the crop ceases early. This may be due to quick loss of moisture from the compost and casing soil. Before casing, the casing soil can be wetted in the normal way though the moisture level as a whole may be little lower. After casing, the bed temperature is kept at 30°C and high humidity should be maintained by watering the bed regularly and by keeping the wall and floor of the spawn running room wet. It was found advantageous to roughen the surface of the casing layer superficially, 6 or 7 days after casing.

After 10 to 12 days, when the mycelium has reached the casing soil, the temperature should be lowered. By starting the ventilation, the temperature can be brought down to 25°C. It is believed that the requirement of fresh air for *A. bitorquis* is less than that of *Agaricus bisporus.* The quantity of fresh air can be adjusted according to the size of the flush. The regular spray of water stimulates the pin head formation. In most cases the fruit body is abnormal in the first flush. The first flush is heavy in this species and this may be due to the relatively high bed temperature during the mycelial growth and after casing. During growth, due to less ventilation, evaporation may be less. For this, the moisture of casing layers should be regularly checked, as high temperature and high humidity may be conducive to many diseases such as bacterial spot and blotches which may cause heavy damage. If the cut surface of the stem turns brown and if many pin heads die it shows that the casing layer is too wet.

Harvesting

As the time period between the button and open stage is quite short, it is advisable to pluck the mushroom at the proper time. As this mushroom requires high concentration of carbon dioxide and high temperature for its growth, one feels uncomfortable at the harvesting time, so before and during plucking, ventilation and circulation can be temporarily raised.

As the temperature requirement of *Agaricus bitorquis* is high, it is quite congenial for false truffle (*Diehliomyces microspora*) bacterial blotch and pits, etc., to make their appearance.

False truffle (*Diehliomyces microspora*)

The spores of this fungus are naturally present in the compost or casing soil. The spores germinate at temperatures 27 to 28°C. In the beginning, the mycelium goes deep in the compost and then in the casing soil. The mycelium is yellowish in colour and slowly it replaces the mycelium of *Agaricus bitorquis* and hence, there is no fruiting of the mushroom. The fruit body of the fungus is like shelled nuts of calves' brain and when ripe they become reddish brown in colour. In severe infestation of this desease a chlorine odour comes from the room.

Control

a) Compost should be properly pasteurised.

b) From spawning and 8 to 10 days after casing the temperature should not rise beyond 27 to 28°C. In case of serious infection the temperature in the picking period should be below 25°C.

c) Do not use casing soil in which spores of truffle disease are suspected.

d) Young truffle bodies should be collected and burnt before they mature.

e) After the crop, the room should be heated out for 12 hours at 70°C.

f) All the wooden trays and other wooden implements should be treated with 2 per cent formaldehyde at the end of the crop.

Bacterial blotch and pests

Due to high humidity, high temperature and less ventilation the bacterial pathogen *Pseudomonas tolaassi* grow and attack the mushroom. Small rust-coloured patches appear which in a later stage coalesce and turn chocolate, the whole mushroom gets rotten in no time.

In general, stagnation, damp air, with temperature above 15 to 16°C encourage the infection, so the growers are mostly in a fix, as increasing the ventilation, will cause scaling and a higher humidity will promote the bacterial infection.

Control

1) Strict cleanliness in and around the farm.

2) Generous ventilation, too high humidity and fluctuation in temperature should be avoided.

3) After watering, mushrooms should dry as quickly as possible and for this, ample ventilation for a short time after watering and increasing the temperature (if the temperature before watering is lowered down) is beneficial.

4) As a preventive, water which is used for watering should be chlorinated and after watering a solution of 2.5 to 3.0 ml chlorine (5 per cent) water should be sprinkled over the beds.

5) For prevention of bacterial spot between the flushes, the bed can be sprayed with 0.25 to 0.3 per cent formaldehyde solution.

Chapter 8

Cultivation of Paddy Straw Mushroom (*Volvariella* spp.)

Paddy straw mushroom is cultivated in the tropical climates of China and the countries of Southeast Asia. There is no proper record when the cultivation of *Volvariella volvacea* originated, but from available information the cultivation of *V. volvacea* had, perhaps, started before the eighteenth century in China, because it is known as the Chinese mushroom as well as Tributary mushroom, or Nanhua mushroom. It is used as a highly priced delicacy in China and in Southeast Asia wherever the Chinese are resident. It is thought that the cultivation of paddy straw mushroom must have been started by the Buddhist monks of Nanhua temple in China. Buddhist monks were vegetarian and mushroom was one of their favourite items of food.

In India the cultivation of straw mushroom was first tried at Coimbatore and since then, its cultivation has been taken over at other places also. It grows at high temperatures between 30 and 45°C. It can, therefore, be cultivated during the summer months. A variety of materials have been tried for cultivation, e.g., cotton waste, water hyacinth, bagasse, paddy straw, etc.

Three species of *Volvariella* are grown in India, namely, *V. diplasia, V. volvacea* and *V. esculenta.* The most conventional method of cultivation of *Volvariella volvacea* is given in the following paragraph.

Paddy straw which is used should be uncrumpled, not very leafy, not more than one year old and preferably hand threshed. It should be stored at a proper place so that it does not get wet during rain. Paddy straw is made into bundles. The bundles are soaked in water for 18 to 24 hours. Soaking can be done in small tanks and to completely immerse the bundles, bricks or any other heavy weight can be put on the bundles. The bundles are then taken out and excess water drained off. The soaked straw bundles with their butt ends on one side are placed length wise close to each other on a bamboo frame supported on bricks. The number of bundles so placed should be such that it approximates to the length of the straw, to make a square bed. A second layer is made by placing the bundles having the butt ends on the opposite side. An arrangement of this type makes one layer. Small bits of spawn are placed 3 to 4 inches inside the margin, leaving a space of 5 cm to 5.5 cm from each other. A small quantity of arhar or gram dal powder is sprinkled over the spawn bits. The third layer of bundles is placed at right angles to the previous layer, i.e., in a criss-cross fashion, and the fourth layer is placed on the third layer with the opposite butt ends. It is also spawned in the same way. Another layer of the bundles is placed with the butt end at right angles to the previous one. This layer is spawned all over and covered with a thin layer of loose straw. Finally the bed is pressed down (Fig. 8.1a). As much as 350 to 400 g of grain spawn is required for spawning one bed (Garcha, 1980). An addition of 20 ounces of ammonium sulphate and 4 ounces of superphosphate per bed, increases the size of the straw mushroom (Ramakrishnan *et al.,* 1968). The bed is covered with a polythene sheet. Watering depends upon the humidity of the air. Mostly no watering is required for the first 3 or 4 days. Watering of the beds and temperature within the beds are very important factors for the yield of paddy straw mushroom. The bed temperature should remain between 30 and 35°C after spawning. The temperature should not go below 30°C during the growing period. Small buttons start appearing 7 to 10 days after spawning. At that time the polythene sheet should be removed from the bed. They remain in the button stage for 4 to 5 days and then grow into full size. Picking is done by gently twisting the fruiting bodies. The correct stage of picking is, when the volva is about to rupture or is just ruptured (Fig. 8.1b).

Different methods are used for cultivation by different workers. Thomas *et al.* (1943), gave the method of cultivation of *Volvariella esculenta*. The bed was prepared on a raised wooden platform 75 × 75 × 30 cm. Three twist bundles with 10 kg of straw were made. These were soaked in water for 12 hours and placed on the platform in a zigzag manner. The spawn of one bottle was used for these bundles. Spawn bits of 25 mm were placed along the margin of the bed. Often it was covered with the third twist. The entire bed was compacted and watered if necessary, with a rose-can to maintain the moisture of the bed. Then the bed was covered with a polythene sheet. Spawn prepared in rice bran + rice chaff and the granular spawn gave maximum yield.

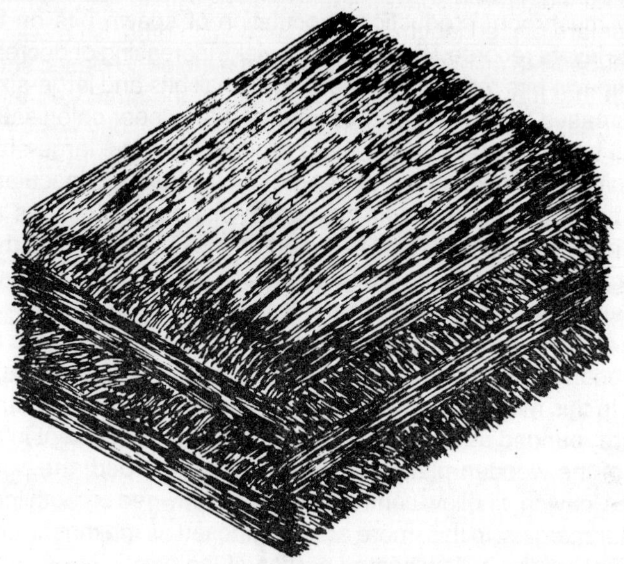

Fig. 8.1(a). Paddy Straw Bed for Cultivation of *Volvariella* Spp.

Fig. 8.1(b). *Volvariella Volvacea* Grown on Paddy Straw Bed.

Spawning the different layers of the bed is an influencing factor in straw mushroom production. Inoculation of spawn bits on the alternate layers recorded the maximum yield. Increasing or decreasing the spawn bits reduced the yield. Too small bits and large-sized bits decreased the yield. This was mostly due to poor colonisation by small bits and crowded pin head production in the large-sized spawn bits, as the pin heads appeared mostly from the inoculated spawn bits. Spacing between the spawn bits also influences the yield. Smaller spacing (5 cm) between small spawn bits (10 mm) and larger spacing (10 mm) between large spawn bits (100 mm) gives better yield (Ramaswamy and Kandaswamy, 1978).

The other method of cultivation of paddy straw mushroom is the hollow bed method described by Krishnamohan and Jaya Rajan (1978). In this method the twists were made with 6 kg paddy straw and were rounded around 30 cm diameter cement pot, kept in the centre of the wooden platform. After pressing the bed, the pot is removed leaving a hollow centre. The bed is spawned on both inner and outer margins. In this, more area is exposed as the mushrooms also appear in the hollow central portion of the bed.

Paddy straw can be grown in polythene bags also as described by Bahl (1982). Chopped paddy straw is soaked in water for 24 hours. Waste paper is cut into small pieces and this is also soaked in water for the same period. After 24 hours excess water is removed from the pulp and paddy straw. Soaked pulp, chopped straw and spawn are mixed thoroughly and filled in the polythene bags. Small holes are made in the polythene bags, for aeration and removal of condensed water. The mouth of the bag is tied with a rubber band and kept at 35 to 40°C. The bag is cut open carefully so that the contents of the bag are not disturbed. A fine spray of water is given twice or thrice in a day according to the climatic conditions to provide 80 to 90 per cent humidity. After 10 to 15 days of spawning the pins start coming up.

Alicbusan (1979) also worked on paddy straw mushroom and the technology developed is for rural area. According to him the beds are made with paddy straw soaked for 3 hours. Crumpled newspapers are soaked in a container with 3 g urea/gallon of water. The soaked paper is planted along with the spawn. The mushroom spawn and soaked paper are distributed on the top of the layer in thumb-sized pieces. The plantings are 5 cm from the edge of the straw and 5 cm apart. The spawn is burried with the paper 4 cm deep in layer. The straw bed is protected by an elevated transparent plastic sheet immediately after the planting. The plastic sheet should be put on a bamboo frame to prevent the moisture that accumulates on the plastic, from spilling on to the straw. Watering is done on each bed frequently according to the air humidity. After 7 to 10 days of spawning the pins come out. More fruiting is found when straw and soil together are used as a substrate.

Similarly, the bed can be made with the dried banana leaves, still hanging on the plant. Such leaves are gathered and cut in uniform length and soaked in water for 3 to 4 hours. A leaf bed is made in the same manner as that of straw. No water should be given for the first 5 days after the bed preparation. During the dry season the bed may be watered gently but generously on the 6th and 7th day after spawning. This should be repeated once a day until the pin heads have developed. More water is sprinkled along the side of the bed. In rainy season when mushrooms are in the pin head stage the bed should not be watered. It should be done only when the mushrooms reach the size of corn seeds and the beds have become somewhat dry. The harvest usually lasts for 3 consecutive days. 5 to 7 days after the first flush another crop is harvested.

For a standard four metre, six-layered bed, a harvest of 7 kg of buttons or 12.6 kg of fully matured mushrooms can be obtained. The straw is soaked until it becomes dark brown in colour or until the banana leaves exhibit a certain degree of transparency. Chua and Ho (1973) grew paddy straw mushroom on banana leaves and saw dust. According to them, paddy straw is soaked in water for 24 hours and the excess water is drained off. A bed of soil (1.8 m × 0.6 m × 0.3 m) is made and two or three layers of soaked straw are piled on the soil bed. About 80 g rice bran is sprinkled evenly on the soil and on each layer of the soaked straw. The straw bed is covered with a polythene sheet and left for a week for composting. After one week the polythene sheet is removed and each layer is inoculated with spawn at the edge at regular intervals. A thin layer of soil is used as a casing layer to cover the inoculated paddy straw. A temporary shed is made over each bed to protect it from direct sunlight and rain.

Volvariella spp. can also be grown in winter. The only care taken is to maintain the temperature of the bed. As the atmospheric temperature is low, the bed temperature will also be low. Hence, the bed temperature is increased by incorporating leaf materials like tamarind, neem, etc., which can be used fresh or partially dried (Ramaswamy and Kandaswamy, 1978). Three twist bundles with 10 kg paddy straw are made after soaking for 12 hours. One twist bundle is arranged in a zigzag manner and 1 kg neem and tamarind leaves are separately spread on this layer. Another layer of twist bundle is put over it and spawned after sprinkling 25 g of red gram powder. The third layer of twisted bundle is put in a zigzag manner to cover the bed. The bed is compacted and covered with transparent polythene sheet. Chang (1978) used cotton waste as a heating material. Cotton waste compost consists of first grade dropping waste (sometimes mixed with card fly, butterfly and oil sweepings), 4 per cent rice or wheat bran, and about 4 to 6 per cent ground agricultural limestone to bring the pH to the required level. The compost can also be made of cotton waste and rice straw in ratios of 2 : 1 or 1 : 1 which is mixed with 3 to 4 per cent limestone. These mixtures are soaked thoroughly in water and heaped on concrete floors to make piles about 1.5 × 1.5 × 1.5 metres which are fermented for 2 to 4 days, depending on the materials used. The piles should be turned over at least once during fermentation. After fermentation, peak heating is done as described in the following paragraph.

The compost is brought in the mushroom house having two tiers of 5 beds each made of iron frame and covered with 4 mm thick polythene film. The roof of the house is of straw mats or any such material. The beds are filled deep with compost and steam is passed into the house through pipes to raise the temperature to 60°C within 2 to 4 hours. This temperature is maintained for 2 hours after which by introducing fresh air by the ventilation system, the temperature is brought down to 52°C and maintained for 8 hours. The temperature is further reduced to 35°C within 8 to 12 hours and then spawning is done. As reported by Chang (1978) this method gives a stable yield.

Diseases and pests

Often weed fungi like *Coprinus aratus, Psathyrella* spp. appear in the beds. Moulds like *Aspergillus* spp., *Rhizopus stolonifer, Sclerotinia rolfsii,* etc., also contaminate the beds which result in a lower yield of the mushroom. Spraying with captan or zineb suppresses the growth of the weed fungi without affecting the crop of straw mushroom. Fumigation of the straw by dow fume C2-arnate has been found useful for the control of weed mushroom (Madic and Roldan, 1965).

Bahl and Chowdhry (1981) reported *Podospora faurelii* as a competitor of *Volvariella volvacea.* This fungus completely inhibits the growth of the mushroom. It attacks paddy straw and causes inhibition in the growth of *Volvariella volvacea. Dactylaria thaumasia,* reported by Chowdhry and Bahl (1980), is a nematophagus fungus and attacks the paddy straw and reduces the yield.

Rotting of button is caused by different organisms, viz., fungus (*Sclerotium* sp.) reported by Muthukrishnan (1971) bacteria by Kannaiyan (1974).

Collembola infestation of *V. diplasia* is reported by Muthukrishnan and Prasad (1971). Muthukrishnan (1971) reported the damage of mushroom by a mite *Scheloribates* sp. and Lepidopterous insect, *Amata* sp. Infestation of the mushroom bed with nematode *Rhabdetis* sp. is also reported by him. Heavy damage by garden snail on *V. diplasia* was reported by Kannaiyan (1974).

A combination spray of an insecticide, a fungicide and an antibiotic, viz., malathion 0.025 per cent + dithane Z-78 or benlate 0.025 per cent will minimise the disease and pest problems (Kannaiyan and Prasad, 1978). The following points are important for a good yield of paddy straw mushroom:

1) *Size of the bed*: This is very important because a small bed will dry too quickly, while in a big bed, temperature will rise beyond the optimum temperature required for growth. Different workers reported different bed sizes to be suitable; e.g., Krishnamurthy and Lalita Kumari (1966) reported the suitable bed size to be about 1 m × 1 m × 1 m. Gupta *et al.* (1970) recommended a bed size of about 1/2 m × 1/2 m × 1/4 m and Aggarwala (1973) gave the optimum bed size as 1/2 m × 1/2 m × 0.6 m.

2) *Amount of spawn and spacing:* Garcha (1980) recommended 350 to 400 g grain spawn/sqm bed size. Chang (1978) reported the spawning rate to be different for different strains, e.g., in the case of strain HK1, it is 0.4 to 0.6 per cent wet substrate by weight, while for HK2, it is 3 to 6 per cent. Spawning in a single layer recorded less yield than spawning in two or three layers. Increasing the spawn load induced profuse pin head formation and poor crop. As the productive pin heads appear directly from the spawn, the spawn may be used as small bits at minimal distances to get a good mushroom crop.

A smaller bit of spawn with less spacing or a greater bit of spawn with more spacing gives good yield. Ramasamy and Kandaswamy (1978) reported good yield with 10 mm spawn and 5 cm spacing or 100 mm spawn bit with 10 cm spacing.

3) *Atmospheric temperature* : Atmospheric temperature should not go below 30°C at any time during the growth period.

Schedule for growing paddy straw mushroom worked out by Garcha (1980) under Punjab conditions is:

1) Preparation of paddy straw bundles—23 April.
2) Wetting the straw bundles for 20 to 24 hours—24 April.
3) Laying of beds and spawning—25 April.

4) Picking—5 May to 19 May.

5) Removal of used straw and general cleaning of the site—20 May.

Similarly 3 more crops can be taken, provided the beds are laid on 22 May, 1 June and 20 July for the second, third and fourth crop respectively. Thus the all summer mushroom growers can have a good crop.

Preservation

Paddy straw mushroom has very little shelf life. It is consumed fresh but it can be preserved either by dehydration or canning.

Mushrooms grown under low light intensity (4–14 lux) have the longer shelf life by 4 hours than those produced under normal diffused light conditions (Kaul, 1978).

Fresh mushroom must be consumed immediately after harvest. If it is preserved at a low temperature (10 to 15°C), it can be kept well for about 48 hours. If the mushrooms are immersed in 10 per cent brine followed by drying in the air they can go well up to one week. Mushroom should be washed well before use to remove salt. Mushroom can be preserved by dehydration. Drying is done either in the sun (the most conventional method) or at a temperature of 55 to 60°C. Fresh mushrooms are reduced to one-eighth their original weight after dehydration. Dried mushrooms can absorb water from the atmosphere, so they should be packed either in aluminium foil or in polythene bags. If they are not dried properly they give a foul smell which, however, goes off during cooking. Dry mushrooms can be powdered and can then be used in making soup, ketchup or curry after re-consumption of water (Su and Seth, 1940).

Canning

Straw mushroom can be canned if it is picked up at a very early button stage. Mushrooms are trimmed, cut to the desired size, washed well in water, blanched for 4 to 5 minutes in boiling water, cooled rapidly to room temperature and filled in tins with 2 per cent hot brine. Cans are sealed and steam sterilised at 10 1b pressure for 40 minutes. After sterilisation the cans are cooled in water and kept in a cool place.

Economics of Production of Paddy Straw Mushroom (Information Collected From Seasonal Grower) Jandaik, 1995

A. *Fixed Costs*	Nil
B. *Variable Costs*	
i) Costs of 30 quintals of paddy straw at Rs. 50/– quintal	1,500.00
ii) Cost of 170 spawn bottles at Rs. 8/– each	1,360.0
iii) Fungicides/insecticides	100.00
iv) Labour (50 mandays) changes at Rs. 30/day	1,500.00
v) Electricity, water, etc.	250.00
vi) Miscellaneous charges including marketing of produce	500.00
	Total : 5,218.00
Anticipated yield at 12% conversion on dry weight basis of substrate	360 kg
Cost of production per kg	Rs. 14.5
Income from sale at Rs. 20/kg	7,200.00
Net profit from one crop	1,982.00

Chapter 9

Cultivation of *Pleurotus* spp.

The oyster mushroom (species of *Pleurotus* genus) grows under natural conditions on trees or dead woody branches of trees as saprophytes and primary decomposers. This mushroom is also known as "Wood fungus" and in India it is commonly known as "Dhingri". It is used in the preparation of many delicious dishes. In India, Bano and Srivastava (1962), and Jandaik and Kapoor (1974) have successfully cultivated the *Pleurotus* spp.

The following species have been cultivated so far:

Pleurotus ostreatus

P. flabellatus

P. sajor caju

P. eryngii

P. sapidus

P. cornucopiae

The cultivation of *Pleurotus flabellatus* has been tried on wheat, ragi and rice straw (Bano *et al.,* 1979). The highest yield was obtained on rice straw. Jandaik and Kapoor (1976) could cultivate *Pleurotus sajor caju* on farm waste products such as banana pseudostems, paddy or wheat straw compost and saw dust. Good yields were obtained with banana pseudostems and chopped paddy straw. The addition of nutrients like oat meal to the substrate gave better yield. The nutritive value of *P. sajor caju*, as given by Jandaik and Kapoor (1975) and *P. flabellatus* by Bano *et al.* (1963), is as follows:

	Pleurotus flabellatus
Ash	0.974%
Crude fibre	1.084%
Fat	0.105%
Moisture	90.95%
Non protein nitrogen	0.14%
Protein	2.75%

Pleurotus sajor caju (Jandaik and Kapoor, 1975) on dry weight basis:

Ascorbic acid	0.06%
Fat	2.26%
Protein	47.93%
Reducing sugars	0.285%
Starch	0.120%

Method of cultivation

There are several methods of cultivation of *Pleurotus* spp. with only little difference or modification.

The method of cultivation of *Pleurotus flabellatus* devised by Bano *et al.* (1974), is as follows:

Dried paddy straw was chopped into 1 to 2 cm long bits and soaked in water overnight. Excess water was drained off and horse gram powder (8 g/kg) and spawn (30 g/kg) were added and mixed with the wet straw. Polyethylene bags with holes were then filled with the foresaid mix (substrate) and kept in a room at 21 to 35°C with sufficient light and ventilation. The mycelium took 11 to 14 days to permeate the substrate in the bags. During this period, the temperature of the substrate varied between 32 and 36°C and later became almost constant at 25 to 28°C with the appearance of mushroom pins on the upper side. The polyethylene bags were cut open on the upper side and on the sides without disturbing the bed, which had become quite compact by then (Figs. 9.1a, b). Water was sprayed over it twice a day. In 3 to 4 days, the crop started coming up (Fig. 9.2).

Besides polyethylene bags, cylindrical beds were also made on circular metallic stands. The stand had 4 legs (each 10 cm long) and 2 metallic rings having a diameter of 8 and 40 cm connected together, by a ½ cm sq wire mesh. Connected to the inner ring, there were 4 iron rods (each 12 cm long and 0.5 cm in diameter) which were supported on an asbestos pipe of 1.6 metre length and 10 cm diameter having 4 vertical rows of holes, each hole being 1 cm in diameter 10 cm apart. The polyethylene tube (40 cm in diameter) with perforations, was placed on the stand around the asbestos pipe. The straw mixed with nutrient and spawn, was stuffed into the space between the polyethylene tube and the asbestos pipe which gave a cylindrical shape to the bed. The asbestos pipe, besides giving a support to the cylindrical beds had a secondary function of expelling heat from the centre of the bed. After the mycelial ramification, through the substrate, straw became a bound

Fig. 9.1(a). Chopped Paddy Straw mixed with Spawn of *Pleurotus* sp. in Polyethylene Bag.

Fig. 9.1(b). Compact Structure after Stripping off the Polyethylene Bag.

Fig. 9.2. ***Pleurotus*** **sp. Grown in Bags.**

mass of compact straw.

The beds, in bags as well as on the circular stands were placed in a well-ventilated room with normal conditions of temperature, relative humidity and light. The temperature range is 20 to 32°C with relative humidity 35 to 75 per cent. It took 12 to 15 days for the completion of mycelial ramification throughtout the substrate whether in bag beds or cylindrical beds. The young sporophores appeared through the holes of the polyethylene sheets. At this stage the polyethylene sheets were cut open, removed and the beds were watered 2 to 3 times a day for 3 days and a relative humidity of 65 per cent ± 5 was maintained during the cropping period. The mushrooms were harvested from the 4th day onwards. Supplementation of mushroom beds with cotton seed powder (132 g/kg dry straw) after the spawn run, increased the yield by 85 per cent. This also improved the texture and flavour of the mushroom.

Another method of cultivation of *P. flabellatus* reported by Bano *et al.* (1979) is as follows:

Preparation of spawn

Paddy straw was chopped as mentioned earlier and treated by hot water at 65 ± 5°C for 10 to 15 minutes, followed by soaking in cold water for 2 hours. Excess water was drained off till the moisture content of the straw was about 80 per cent. Horse gram powder (1 per cent) and spawn (3 per cent) (W/W) were added and mixed. This inoculated substrate was filled (about 4 to 5 kg/bag) in polyethylene bags, 53 cm × 85 cm having 25 holes of 1 cm diameter, 7 cm apart on either side of the bag. The bags were tied and placed in well ventilated room for 15 days. This was used as substrate spawn.

Cultivation

Paddy straw was fumigated with methyl bromide fumes at the rate of 64 mg/litre of atmosphere for 48 hours. The straw was then chopped as before, soaked in water for 18 hours and excess water was drained off. Horse gram powder 1 per cent and substrate spawn 10 per cent (by weight of the substrate) was added and mixed with the wet straw. The mix (1.5 kg/bag) was then filled in the polyethylene bags 38 × 26 cm with 72 holes (1 cm diameter) on either side. The rest of the procedure was the same as described earlier.

Tewari and Sohi (1979) suggested the cultivation of *Pleurotus sajor caju* on paddy straw and maize stalk (1:2). These were soaked in water for 20 hours. Excess water was drained off and mixed with 4 per cent (W/W) rice bran. The mix was filled in earthen pots, spawned and was covered with paper. On the appearance of small pin heads, the paper was removed and a little heavier watering was done. The relative humidity, 70 to 80 per cent could be maintained by spraying water on walls and floors.

Chakrabarty and Sarkar (1978) grew *P. sajor caju* in beds. 1.25 cm thick layer of straw is placed in soil beds (60 × 15 cm) surrounded by 15 cm high × 20 cm wide soil bunds). N.P.K. (15 : 15 : 15) is mixed in the lower layer of paddy straw and spawning is done at the rate of 1 bottle per 0.72 sq metre. Spawn is covered with 1.25 cm layer of soaked straw, casing is done simultaneously. For casing, soil can be collected from 6" depth. Unsterilised casing soil is used and pins start coming after 20 to 25 days of spawning. The yield is 2600 g fresh mushroom/kg of dry straw.

Bano and Srivastava (1962) gave the method of cultivation of *Pleurotus* spp. Fresh dried paddy straw was cut and made into bundles of about 1', long, soaked in water overnight and used to make the beds on a raised platform with slight inclination on one side, to avoid stagnation of water. The straw was spread in thin layers in a space of 1 sq ft and the spawn bits were distributed along the periphery 2" apart. The nutrient oat meal, or Bengal gram 6 g/bed was sprinkled over the spawn bits and was covered with another layer

Fig. 9.3 *Pleurotus sajor caju* Grown in Basket.

Fig. 9.4 *Pleurotus sajor caju* Grown in Wooden Trays.

of straw crosswise. This was repeated thrice till the bed attained a thickness of 4 layers of spawn and 5 layers of straw. The beds were pressed slightly in order to bring the spawn in contact with the substrate and were watered thrice a day to keep them moist and kept under the shade. The temperature was 21 to 35°C with 67 to 72 per cent relative humidity.

Pleurotus spp. can be grown in any container, e.g., earthen pot, cane basket, polyethylene bags, iron baskets or in wooden trays as shown in the photographs (Figs. 9.2, 9.3 and 9.4).

Economics of *Pleurotus* cultivation in hills on a small scale (with hot water treatment) Jandaik, 1995

A. *Fixed Cost*	
i) Land already available with the grower	
ii) Cost of construction of mud-thatched house (60' × 20' × 12') of one thousand bags capacity	9,000.00
iii) Cost of racks	2,500.00
iv) Cost of spray pump, thermometer, forks and knives	2,000.00
v) Cost of two drums/tubs	800.00
	Total : 14,300.00/-
B. *Variable Cost*	
i) Cost of 5 quintals of wheat straw at Rs. 100/ quintal	500.00
ii) Cost of polythene bags	350.00
iii) Cost of 100 spawn bags at Rs. 8/bag	800.00
iv) Insecticides/pesticides	150.00
v) Cost of fuel/wood for boiling water	250.00
vi) Miscellaneous charges including marketing expenses	500.00
	Total : 2,550.00/-
C. *Depreciation and Interest*	
i) Depareciation of 5% and interest at 12% on A for 2 months	405.00
ii) Total expenditure (B + C)	2,955.00
iii) Anticipated yield at 63% B.E. (biological efficiency)	315 kg
iv) Cost of production per kg	Rs. 9.4
v) Income from sale at Rs. 25/kg	7,875.00
vi) Net profit from one crop (income - expenses)	4,920.00

Chapter 10

Common Edible Mushrooms of India

Agaricus arvensis Schaeff ex Seer

Syn. *Psalliota arvensis* (Schaeff ex Seer) Kummer.

It is found in lawns, meadows, cultivated fields, and in pastures, etc., either solitary or scattered.

Pileus is smooth, white or yellowish, convex or conical, bell shaped.

Distribution: Calcutta, Baroda, Nagpur.

Agaricus bisporus (Lange) Sing.

Growing on manure heaps, in the soil, in gardens, and green houses. Pileus, convex when young and flattened when old. Whitish to light brown.

Distribution: Solan, Himachal Pradesh.

Agaricus campestris L. ex Fr.

Syn. *Psalliota campestris* (L. ex Fr.) Quel.

This is the widest known of all mushrooms. It is found in fields, pastures and in manured ground. Pileus is globular when young, convex to flattened at maturity. Surface dry, downy, even quite scaly. Varying in colour from creamy white to light brown.

Distribution: Punjab, Calcutta, West Bengal, Bihar, North Western Himalayas, Nagpur, Jammu.

Agrocybe praecox (Bull. ex st. Amans Fayod.)

Syn. *Phliota praecox* (Pers.) Fr.

It is found in open woods, lawns, pastures or on the ground either single or in groups.

Pileus, convex when young and expanded when old. It is whitish umbo or yellowish at first, later changes to yellowish-brown.

Margin slightly turned inside at the young stage but later turns upward. Sometimes surface is uneven with many shallow pits.

Distribution: Saharanpur, Uttar Pradesh.

Amanita caesaria (Scop. ex Fr.) Pers. ex Schw.

This is the orange amanita. It is large and attractive. Pileus is smooth, hemispherical, bell shaped, convex and at maturity it is flat and the margin slightly curved downwards, red or orange, fading to yellow on the margin. Usually the large and well-developed specimen have a deeper and richer colour, the colour being always more marked in the centre of the pileus. The annulus yellow or orange hanging down upon the stem like a collar.

At button stage the white-coloured volva surrounds the stipe, when the mushroom matures, the volva ruptures and orange coloured pileus comes out.

Distribution: Baroda, Khasi hills, Assam.

Amanita vaginata (Bull. ex Fr.) Vitt.

Syn. *Amanitopsis vaginata* (Bull. ex Fr.) Roze.

It is edible but should be used with great caution. It is quite variable in colour, ranging from white to mouse colour, brownish or yellowish.

The pileus is ovate at first, bell shaped, convex and expanded, thin, quite fragile, smooth when young, with a few fragments of volva adhering to its surface. Volva is long, thin, fragile, forming a permanent sheath which is quite soft and readily adheres to the base of the stem.

It is found in woods, in open places where there is much vegetable mould, sometimes found in stubble and pastures, especially in meadows under trees.

Distribution: Below Nunklow, Khasi hills, Assam, Solan, Nagpur.

Armillaria mellea (Vahl ex Fr.) Kummer

It is found either solitary, gregarious or in dense clusters. This grows either in thin woods or on cleared lands, on the ground, on dead trees or at the base of the old tree stumps.

Cap fleshy, honey coloured or ochraceous, striate on the margin, shaded with darker brown towards the centre. Sometimes a central depression is found in full-grown specimens, tufted with dark brown fugitive hair. Colour of the cap varies, depending upon climatic conditions and the character of the habitat. The veil varies greatly. It may be membranous and thin, or quite thick or may be wanting entirely.

Distribution: Baroda, Deoban, Jaunsar, Uttar Pradesh.

Bovista plumbea Pers.

The mushroom is quite small, grows on the ground, in old pastures, being quite plentiful after warm rains. Sporophores grow in humiculous soil or in old pastures without anchoring rhizoids and at maturity freeing from the substrate. Whitish, glabrous. When young, splitting irregularly into white granules and finally falling off. Peridium lead coloured, papery, having small narrow mouth, gleba at first white, then red, finally dark brown to purple, powdery.

Distribution: Arnigadh, Mussoorie, Sonamarg, Kashmir, Khadrala, Himachal Pradesh.

Calvatia cyathiformis (Bose) Morg.

Sporophores growing in groups on soil, grassy land and sometimes on the cultivated fields. Sometimes solitary on sandy soil. White when young but turning into brown with pinkish tinge at maturity. Peridium breaks into irregular fragments.

Distribution: Ahmedabad, Gujarat, Gurdaspur, Punjab.

Calvatia utriformis (Bull. ex Pers.) Toap.

Syn. *Calvatia caelata* (Ball.) Morg.

Calvatia bovista (Pers.) Kambly and Lee.

Sporophores growing solitary or scattered on the ground, in meadows, pastures or grassy lands. Peridium large, ovoid or top shaped, depressed above, with a stout thick base and cord-like root. Whitish at first, yellow or brown when old, surface covered with warty patches, spines or cracks.

Distribution: Himachal Pradesh, Bashahr state, Babeh pass.

Cantharellus cibarius Fr.

It grows in woods and in rather open places. It is of a rich egg yellow colour. The pileus is fleshy, at first convex, later flat, depressed in the centre, finally funnel shaped, bright to deep yellow, firm smooth but often irregular. Its margin often wavy, flesh white, the cap has the appearance of an inverted cone.

Distribution: West Bengal, Kashmir, Mussoorie, Arnigadh, Solan, Himachal Pradesh.

Coprinus atramentarius (Bull ex Fr.) Fr.

This grows very abundantly in dense clusters on damp rich ground, gardens, rich lawns, and dumping grounds. The pileus is at first egg shaped, grey or greyish brown, first smooth except that there is a slight scaly appearance, margin ribbed, often notched, soft when it melts away in inky fluid.

Distribution: Allahabad, Uttar Pradesh, Kashmir valley.

Coprinus comatus (Mill ex Fr.) S.F. Gray.

Sporophores growing singly, scattered or in clusters on grassy land, in lawns, gardens, fields, on roadside and on refuse dumps. The pileus is fleshy, moist, at first egg shaped, cylindrical, becoming bell shaped, seldom expanded, splitting at the margin along the line of the gills, scattered yellowish scales, tinged with purplish black, sometimes entirely white, surface shaggy. At maturity pileus become an inky fluid.

Distribution: West Bengal, Calcutta, Baroda, Punjab, U.P. and several other parts of India, Bombay, Darjeeling, Kashmir valley, Nagpur.

Coprinus micaceus (Bull. ex Fr.) Fr.

Sporophore growing usually in dense clumps or more or less scattered on ground, sometimes at the base of the living trees or around stumps, rarely on logs in woods. Pileus is ovate when young, turning yellow, tan or light buff, ovate, bell shaped, glistening mica-like scales covering undisturbed young specimen.

Distribution: Calcutta, Srinagar, Nagpur.

Flammulina velutipes (Curt. ex Fr.) Karst

Syn. *Colybia velutipes* (W. curt ex Fr.) Kummer.

Sporophores growing in clumps on dead wood, or on old stumps and in decaying wood either erect or prostrate. Several fruit bodies emerge from the common rooting structure. Pileus flattened, orange to tawny, surface glabrous, margin inrolled. The lower half of the stipe is covered with dense reddish-brown hair giving a velvety appearance, without annulus and volva.

Distribution: Calcutta, Darjeeling, Sikkim, Kulu, Punjab.

Heterobasidion annosum (Fr.) Br.

Syn. *Fomes annosus* (Fr.) Cke

Polyporus annosus Fries

Polyporus irregularis Undrew

Sporophores growing solitary or imbricate on stumps and logs, among coniferous trees or among hard wood. Pileus is sessile often larger, greyish brown when young but dark brown when old, occasionally blackish, tough and corky when fresh, hard after drying.

Distribution: Deoban, Jaunsar, U.P., shillong, Assam, Bedyar, Chakra, Kulu, Punjab, Bashahr, Himachal Pradesh, the Himalayas.

Hirneola auricular judae (Bull. pet St. Amans) Berk.

Syn. *Auricularia auricula*—judae (L.) Schroet.

Auricularia auricula (L. ex Hooker) Underwood.

The Jews Ear: It is gelatinous, 1 to 4 inches across, thin, concave, wavy, flexible when moist, hard when dry, blackish, fuzzy, hairy beneath. It looks like ears. It grows on dead wood and logs or on tree trunks.

Distribution: Calcutta, Sikkim, the Himalayas, Khandala, Bomaby, Kashmir.

Hydnum sepandum L. ex Fr.

Syn. *Dentinum sepandum*

The usual colour of the cap is buff, sometimes very pale, almost white. The colour and smoothness of the cap have given the name of "doe skin mushroom". It is variable in size and colour, growing solitary or in clusters. The cap is fleshy, brittle, convex or nearly plane, colour varying from a pale buff to a distinct brick red, flesh creamy white, inclining to turn brown when bruised, taste slightly aromatic, margin often wavy.

Distribution: Arnigadh, Uttar Pradesh, Himachal Pradesh.

Laccaria laccata (Scop. ex Fr.) Cooke.

Syn. *Clitocybe laccata* Scop.

Sporophores usually growing singly, sometimes scattered in clumps on ground or on rotten wood, in fields, forests and other waste places.

Pileus is convex when young, expanded or flattened at maturity, sometimes funnel shaped, salmon or purple coloured when fresh, pale yellow when moist, light coloured when dry, surface smooth or with minute scales, thin watery appearance.

Distribution: Arnigadh, Mussoorie, Uttar Pradesh, Sikkim.

Lactiporus sulphureus (Bull. ex Fr.) Murr

Syn. *Polyporus sulphureus* (Bull.) Fr.

Boletus sulphureus Bull.

It grows on decayed logs, on stumps and on decayed places, and on living trees.

Cap: In mature stage the growth is horizontal and spreading fan like from stem. Upper surface is salmon, orange or orange red. Flesh cheesy, light yellow, the edge being smooth and unevenly thickened with nodule like prominence.

Distribution: Shillong, Assam, Sikkim, Kashmir, Bashahr, H.P., Chakrata, U.P.

Leucocoprinus cepaestipes (Sow. ex Fr.) Patouillard.

Syn. *Lepiota cepaestipes* (Sow.) Quel.

Sporophores usually growing in partial fairy rings in soil, freshly manured ground or sometimes in decomposed vegetable matter or in saw dust, on logs, rotten wood.

Fruiting body with powdery veil and collapsing at maturity. Pileus ovate when young, latter expanded or broadly conical with an umbo, usually white but umbo often appear brownish, thin, surface dry.

Distribution: Calcutta, Baroda, Uttar Pradesh, Poona, Bombay.

Lycoperdon perlatum Pers.

Syn. *Lycoperdon gemmatum.*

Sporophores are solitary, or scattered on the ground, in open places or in forests, sometimes on rotten wood, usually small.

There are long, thick, erect spine or warts or irregular shape, with the smaller ones in between, whitish or grey in colour, sometimes with a tinge of red brown colour. First the larger spines fall away.

Distribution: North Western Himalayas, Dalhousie, Punjab, Jabalpur, Darjeeling, Sikkim, the Himalayas, Himachal Pradesh.

Lycoperdon pyriformin Pers.

It grows in dense cluster. Puff balls are pear shaped. The surface is covered with minute brownish scales or granules which are persistent. The body is first white, then greenish, yellow and olivaceous. Puff balls are sessile or small stem is present, at the base there are mycelium threads.

Distribution: Kulu, Kashmir, Sonamarg, Sikkim.

Macrolepiota mostoidea (Fr.) Singer

Syn. *Lepiota mastoidea* (Fr.) Kummer

Sporophores growing in fields. Campanulate when young, then convex and later becoming umbonate, white surface with greyish or brownish appressed scales.

Distribution: Calcutta, Hooghly, West Bengal, Uttar Pradesh.

Macrolepiota procera (Scop. ex Fr.) Sing.

Syn. *Lepiota procera* (Scop. ex Fr.) S.F. Gray

Found in soil, pasture, lawns, woods and gardens. Pileus is thin, strongly umbonate with brown spot-like scales. The stem is very long, cylindrical, hollow or stuffed, even very long in proportion to its thickness. The ring is thick and firm, at maturity it becomes loosened and movable on stem.

Distribution: Calcutta, Uttar Pradesh, Saharanpur, Lucknow.

Morchella conica Pers.

Sporophores scattered on the ground in forest. Buff or yellow when young, darker when old. It is conical in shape, Cap pointed, pits arranged in rows usually longer than broad, sometimes irregular. Ridges extend longitudinally and run parallel from base to the top.

Distribution: Dehradun, Siwalik hills, Himachal Pradesh.

Morchella deliciosa Fr.

Cap is cylindrical with blunt top. Stipe is short and is hollow from top to the bottom. It is found in wood borders, also in old apple and peach orchards. Pits usually narrow, elongated.

Distribution: Amritsar, Kashmir, Kumaon hills, the Himalayas, U.P., Himachal Pradesh.

Morechella esculenta ex St. Amans.

Sporophores usually solitary on the ground, under trees in open woods, grassy land, road sides, clay soil, old apple and peach orchards. It has a cap little longer than broad and is almost oval in shape. Sometimes it is nearly round but again it is often slightly narrowed in its upper half, but not pointed or cone like. Pits are irregularly arranged.

Distribution: Punjab, Kashmir, Chamba, Kumaon hills, the Himalayas, Himachal Pradesh.

Pleurotus flabellatus (Berk and Br.) Sacc.

Sporophores grow on dead tree trunk or on ground. Base of sporophores sponge like, fruit body short, fan shaped, first pink and then white.

Distribution: Calcutta, Mysore.

Pleurotus ostreatus (Jacquin ex Fr.) Kummer

Syn. *Pleurotus salignus* (Pers. ex Fr.) Kummer

This usually grows in clusters on dead tree trunks or branches, rarely on living trees.

Sporophores are ostreate white, grey or sometimes yellowish after drying, surface smooth, margin incurved, stipe short, sometimes hairy at the base.

Distribution: West Bengal, Baroda, Sonamarg, Kashmir, Jammu.

Pleurotus sajor caju (Fr.) Singer

Syn. *Lentinus sajor caju* Fr.

Sporophores usually grow solitary or in groups on dead, decaying plants. It is oyster-shaped, often lobed and folded at maturity giving a coralloid appearance, white to grey or dull brown in colour, surface smooth, margin irregular and incurved.

Distribution: South Andaman Island, Hooghly district, West Bengal, foothills of the Himalayas.

Podabrella microcarpa

Syn. *Entoloma microcarpum* Ber and Br.

Termitomyces microcarpus (Berk and Br.)

Sporophores growing solitary, occurring in large numbers on termite nests or on soil, usually small. Pileus small with central acute umbo, flattened, pink at the margin and olive brown at the umbo, surface smooth.

Distribution: Calcutta, West Bengal, Madras.

Psathyrella hydrophilum (Bull. ex Merat)

Syn. *Hypholoma appendiculata* Bull.

Psathyrella candolleana (Fr.)

Sporophores usually scattered or clustered on old tree stumps or logs and sometimes on earth, very fragile, fruiting body not becoming a black fluid. Pileus usually appears white or brown, pale when old, surface smooth or sometimes covered with numerous, white, delicate scales, fleshy and thin, sometimes cracking irregularly or splitting into lobes when old.

Distribution: Baroda, Saharanpur, Uttar Pradesh.

Rigidoporus ulmarius (Sow. or Fr.) Imaz.

Syn. *Fomes geotropus* Cooke

Polyporus (Fomes) *geotropus* Cooke

Sporophores growing solitary imbricate on dead wood of coniferous trees and sometimes on hard wood, soft and fleshy, hard and woody when dry. Body is whitish or buff when fresh, ochraceous on drying.

Distribution: Mundali, Chakrata, Mussoorie, Uttar Pradesh and Western Himalayas.

Russula emetica (Schaeff ex Fr.) S.F. Gray.

Sporophores growing solitary or scattered on the ground in forests, in open places or on rotten wood, fruiting body brittle when broken, lacking milk-like fluid. Pileus convex to camp anulate when young, then expanded, depressed when old, pink to red when young and pale red with age, surface smooth and shining, slightly sticky when young, margin marked with streaks, cuticle easily peeled off. Taste unpleasant.

Distribution: Darjeeling, Khasi hills, Assam.

Russula lepida Fr.

Sporophores growing in mixed forests or in coniferous woods, usually smaller, fruiting body brittle when broken, lacking milk like fluid. Pileus convex at first, later becoming plain, bright red, becoming pale with age, sometimes whitish near the centre, texture silky, surface not shining, cracking when mature.

Distribution: Darjeeling, Kodaikanal, Tamil Nadu.

Chapter 11

Cultivation of *Stropharia rugoso annulata*

Stropharia rugoso annulata was found and described first time in U.S.A., later on in Germany, Czechoslovakia and Japan. It is also called "Garden's Giant" due to its giant size (60 g single fruit body).

Depending on the variety and conditions of growth, the pileus of a mature *Stropharia* attains a diameter of 5–40 cm. The colour of a pileus depends on the variety and on the temperature of the environment. Young fruit bodies are white, they carry characteristic papillae. The colour of pileus of older fruit bodies is yellow or brown with reddish tinge. At low temperature colour of fruit bodies are white. At first lamellae are grey then bluish black. The stipe is whitish cream coloured and having thickened base. In mature fruit bodies the stipe is hollow. The pileus remains at the top of the stipe and velum forms a characteristic ring-like arrangement having a cotton wool consistency around the stipe. Winnetou variety is early variety forming abundant fruit bodies which grow in cluster. It is bright in colour and light in weight. For cultivation this variety is preferred. *Stropharia* is mildly scented and bland in taste.

Cultivation

The cultivation of *Stropharia* is done in warm and semi-sheltered place. Constant shading hinders its development. *Stropharia* is grown on fresh straw of cereal or flax without any supplementation (Fig. 11.1)

Before preparing the bed, straw is moistened. For moistening, straw is arranged in a heap and watered two or three times in a day for 6 to 10 days. When greater amount of straw is being watered, it is necessary to turn over the pile two or three times, straw can also be moistened in a barrel for 48 hrs.

Appropriate moistening of straw prior to planting of spawn,

Fig. 11.1 ***Stropharia*** **sp. Grown on Fresh Straw.**

constitues the basic factor on which the results of cultivation depend. When the mycelia has established, watering of the substrate is destructive.

Layout of beds

Stropharia can be grown in molds or a frame on which foil and roofing paper is stretched to prevent access of earth moles, mice, insects etc. Frame should have slope on one side to keep the rain off.

Moist straw is placed in layers in wooden frames and compressed. The bed should be 25 cm high. To prepare 1 m^2 bed it is necessary to have 20–30 kg dry straw. To get faster growth of mycelium the straw should be thoroughly beaten down. Once a bed is prepared mycelium should be planted immediately.

Production and planting of spawn

The mycelium is grown on moist chaff (2–3 cm long) of wheat or rye. Before inoculation, the chaff is beaten down in glass container which was plugged and then sterilized. After cooling, the chaff was inoculated and kept at 26–27°C to promote growth of the mycelium. After five to six weeks the mycelium cylinder was taken out from the container. Five to six hundred gram spawn is sufficient for 1–1.5 m^2 bed area.

As soon as the bed is prepared, the spawn was planted to a depth of 5–8 cm and the site of planting was pressed down, when the planting is over the bed surface should have even appearance. The planted beds should be covered immediately with the moist newspaper or sacks. During spawn run, the temperature should be between 25–28°C and the beds should not be aerated. Depending on the temperature, the spawn run is over from three to five weeks. After that moist paper is removed and the casing is done. If the upper layer of straw is dry, it should be removed and then casing is done.

Cropping

Covered beds provide conditions for the fusion of hyphae into knots from which the fruit bodies are formed. The characteristic of casing material is that of a casing of button mushroom. Combination of clay or soil with humus of peat is the ideal covering soil. Forest soils both derived from coniferous and broad-leaved forests are also suitable. The pH of the covering soil should be between 5.7–6.0. It is disinfected either by steaming or by Formalin. 10–14 days after casing, the beds require aeration. Fruit bodies are formed four weeks after casing the bed.

At the time of fruit body formation *Stropharia* is not susceptible to temperature fluctuation, only the aeration affects the quality and quantity of the crop. On cooler days, the windows should be closed. More aeration is necessary only when there are large number of fruit bodies on the beds. Watering should be adjusted to the degree of dryness of the cover, never more than 1.5 litres of water to 1 m^2 bed area should be added in a single round. Dry beds require more frequent watering but with small amount of water.

Although *Stropharia* is comparatively resistant to excess water, its infiltration into the substrate is detrimental.

Harvesting

It takes normally 10–12 days for the fruit body to reach the full maturity. Consequently, successive crops come up at the same intervals. Most abundant are first and second crop.

Unlike common mushrooms, *Stropharia* are harvested at full ripeness, when the cortina covering the lamellae is disrupted, yet the pileus remains bell shaped. Latest harvest takes place when the pileus margin are not finelexed and gills are still grey.

Fruit bodies of *Stropharia* are removed out of the covering layer or the beds. They should be gently pressed with two fingers by the pileus irrespective of partial destruction of young fruit bodies growing in the vicinity. Holes remaining after removal of the fruit bodies should be filled up with cover soil. No remains of the fruit body should be left on the bed. The yield of *Stropharia* is about 16 kg/m^2.

Chapter 12

Cultivation of *Auricularia* spp.

(*Jew's ear*)

Auricularia or the jelly fungi is one of the common edible mushroom that grows on decaying wood trunks or logs in forests and backyards.

The fruiting bodies are waxy, cartilagenous and change from purplish brown to black, especially when dry. The common name wood ear, jew's ear or rat's ear is derived from ear like shape of these fruiting bodies. Commercially available spp. are *A. auricula, A. fuscosuccinea* are light coloured and small; while *A. polytricha* is dark coloured, large and hairy and does not turn slimy on cooking. This mushroom is believed to cure sore throat, anaemia, certain disgestive disorders, especially piles on regular consumption. Among the cultivated mushroom, the black ear mushroom is the first which was cultivated in China around 600 A.D. Some of the S.E. Asian countries have started its cultivation for export and home consumption. Its total annual world production has steadily increased (199.07 × 100 metric tonnes) and ranks fifth among the different cultivable mushroom (Chang, 1987). Thailand is a major importer of this mushroom for local use and 90% of dried produce of Taiwan is exported to Hong Kong, Japan and U.S.A.

Auricularia grows in hot and humid climate and its cultivation is being done in China, Taiwan, South Korea, Japan, Thailand, Philippines, etc. Since centuries, it is being cultivated on wooden logs. Except for pines, this mushroom is less specific for the type of wood. The logs are cut in autumn having high moisture content and with high sugar accumulation. The meter long log having a diameter of 3–6 cm is preferred for easy handling. Inoculation of logs is done by making holes in quinquinol fashion and filled with sawdust spawn. The holes are plugged with bark and sealed with wax. Distance between the holes depend on length and diameter of wood (Chang and Tu, 1978).

Diameter of log (cm)	No. of holes chiseled
6	6 or more
9	12 or more in 3 ranks
12	16 or more in 3 or 4 ranks
15	20 or more in 5 ranks
18	24 or more in 6 ranks

The logs are incubated at about 28°C for approximately two months after which it starts cropping.

Laying of logs

Auricularia can grow in a greenhouse, mushroom growing house or in open yard. The inoculated logs are laid crosswise or stand upright in the yard and are covered with plastic sheets or straws to maintain suitable moisture. Logs may also be piled up in an open cellar and covered with tree branches or straws. The length of the vegetative growth period depends upon several factors such as type of wood, vigour of spawn, quantity of inoculum, weather conditions, competition of weed fungi and the physical condition of the laying yard. However, the growth takes about 30–40 days under normal conditions. Logs are turned upside down once a month to keep an even mycelial growth throughout the log and are watered every two to five days, depending upon the environmental conditons. The log surface should always be dry to avoid contamination of weed fungi. It needs no sun light throughout the entire laying period. When the mycelium have fully grown, logs are then transferred to a cropping yard.

Cropping yard

In the cropping yard, the logs are kept upright individually or two logs are arranged in the form of an 'A'. The lower ends of the logs are kept at a distance of about 10 cm to provide space for growing fruit bodies.

Both the temperature and moisture conditions of the cropping yard are very important. Temperature for fruit body formation is 23–28°C. The cropping continued till the suitable temperature prevails in nature. If the logs are protected then one can take harvest every year under natural growing conditions. One piece of Sesbania log (12–15 cm) gives about 3–5 kg (dried) yield in 5–6 months. The total yield expected after several years of cropping will be 10–20% of original weight of log.

Due to scarcity of log, now the cultivation has been started in polythene bags. In bag, cultivation on different substrates like saw-dust, maize stems, cotton seed hulls, corn cobs and paddy straw by supplementations and pasteurization, etc. have been reported by different workers.

Bag method cultivation

The method of cultivation in sawdust was described by Cheng and Tu (1978). *Auricularia* is grown in a special type of house as given in case of *Shiitake.* Sawdust is mixed with 2–20% rice bran to enrich the medium. Sometimes calcium carbonate is added to adjust the pH of the medium. The mixed sawdust is packed in a plastic bag and pressed to form a cylindrical cake. They are sterilized at 90–100°C for 90 minutes. The bags are inoculated after cooling and then transferred to a growing house maintained at 28°C or lower. After the mycelium is fully grown both the ends of the bags are cut off for cropping. The bags are arranged on the growing frames to form piles. The height of the pile is usually about the height of a man for the convenience of picking the fruit bodies. Due to the soft texture of bag and the medium, it is necessary to take special care when moving the bags. Bags should not be broken into pieces, because fruit bodies will never form in broken bags. There are usually only three to four flushes for picking in one cropping and yield of each bag is about 300–500 g. After cropping is complete the bags are moved out immediately.

In case of wheat straw cultivation, the chopped wheat straw is also supplemented with 4% rice bran filled in polypropylene bag and was autoclaved at 15 psi for two hours. After cooling the bags were inoculated with 2% saw dust or grain spawn (on wet weight basis). Grain spawn should be preferably fresh but not beyond one month old. Sawdust spawn can remain viable for 3–4 months of storage.

For spawn run and cropping, the bags can be hung in close proximity (5–7 cm distance). They can be placed on shelves also. Temperature range is 22–28°C and 80 ± 1% R.H. for its mycelial run and cropping. It takes 2–3 weeks for complete spawn run. After that, slitting of the bags were done. Slitting is better than complete removal of bags as it prevents drying. Depending upon the atmospheric humidity, frequency of the watering should be decided. Daily two hours ventilation and light is also necessary for its fruiting. The optimum light intensity of the cropping room varies with the spp. of *Auricularia* (Fig. 12.1).

Harvesting

When young, the mushroom has thick edge resembling a cup which gradually thins out into many margins. This is the actual stage of

Fig. 12.1. Cultivation of *Auricularia* sp. on Wheat Straw.

harvesting. *Auricularia* is less perishable in nature. It can remain on substrate even upto 7–10 days after attaining maturity.

Yin and Nieu (1988) could cultivate *Auricularia* on cotton hull and good yield of 6–8 kg dry mushrooms were produced from 100 kg cotton seed hulls.

Chapter 13

Cultivation of *Flammulina velutipes*

Flammulina velutipes occurs all over the world in areas such as China, Siberia, Asia minor, Europe, Africa, South America, Australia and Japan. It grows on trunks or stumps of aspens, willows and other broad-leaved trees from the end of autumn to early spring. In Japan, it has been used as food for many centuries and cultivated artificially.

Temperature is one of the important factors in the mycelial development and fruit body formation. Generally mycelium grows in the range of 3–4°C to 33–34°C. The optimum temperature is 22–26°C. The mycelium does not die but grows slowly, when exposed to temperature of 3–4°C, at 34°C the growth ceases and over 34°C the mycelium is killed. Primordium formation takes place between 12–20°C and 13°C is the optimum temperature. Following incubation at 20°C for 25 days on sawdust media, when mycelium is exposed to temperature 10 and 15°C it takes 12–14 days for fruiting to occur.

Moisture and humidity is also very important factor for growth of mycelium and fruit body formation. Mycelial growth is fast when the sawdust media has 60–65% moisture. Fruiting and growth of the fruit body are also influenced by the oxygen supply of the cultivation room.

Primordia of *F. velutipes* are induced in the dark, but light is essential for the maturation of the fruit body, without light only rudiments of a fruit body is formed. When light is given during the fruit body formation, the fruit bodies become brown and caps open before the stem fully elongate. Light provided for normal working is sufficient for fruit body initiation.

Cultivation

Flammulina velutipes is cultivated on wooden logs or on sawdust medium. The quality of mushroom grown on wood is inferior. Since white, stiff and durable sporocarp is preferred, its cultivation on sawdust is becoming common now. Fruiting is better in sawdust of *Cryptomeria japonica, C. obtusa* or sawdust of broad leaved trees. Sawdust media have oxygen and water, which is necessary for mycelial growth. Accordingly, growers use sawdust which absorb and hold good quantity of water or they may heap the sawdust for ½ year to 1 year for softening before use. In Japan, mostly sawdust of *C. japonica, C. obtusa* and *Pinus* spp. are widely used for commercial cultivation. Media is prepared by mixing four parts of sawdust with one part of rice bran in a mechanical mixer for 15 min. After adjusting the water content to 50–60% moisture, the media is re mixed.

Polypropelene bottles (800–1000 ml) are widely used as vessels for cultivation and are mechanically filled, approximately 540 g medium/vessel before capping to prevent contamination and drying out.

The filled bottles are autoclaved for 4 hours at 95°C at low pressure and 1 hour at 120°C under high pressure. After the bottles have been sterilized and cooled down to 20°C they are inoculated with sawdust spawn.

Spawn

Sawdust spawn is prepared by mixing ten parts of sawdust with one part of rice bran and enough water to provide a certain degree of humidity. One bottle of spawn (1000 ml) provides sufficient inoculum for 50–60 cultivating bottles.

Spawning and cropping

The optimum temperature for the growth of mycelium is between 22–25°C, the bottles are kept in the room where temperature is maintained between 18–21°C. It takes nearly 20–25 days to cover the whole bottle. When the mycelium spreads to 90% of the bottle space, the cap is pulled off, the inoculated spawn is removed and the surface of the media is made smooth for fruiting.

Bottles are then placed in the dark at a temperature of 10–12°C and humidity is maintained at 80–85%. Moisture level in the bottle is important for fruiting, when the air in bottles get dried up, aerial hyphae appear on the surface of the medium and fruiting is not uniform. On the contrary, when there is too much moisture, amber-coloured water drops form on the surface producing inferior fruit bodies. Good fruit bodies are formed by adjusting the humidity in the room to maintain the correct moisture content of the substrate. Primordia are formed in 10–14 days after low temperature treatment.

At temperature 10–12°C fruit bodies grow rapidly but they are slender, long and of poor quality. The growth of the fruit bodies is controlled by lowering the temperature to 3–5°C and providing air movement (3–5 m/sec) which produce stiff, white and drier fruit bodies. This control is continued for 5–7 days, from the period when the caps differentiation is observed with the naked eyes to the period when the length of the stem reaches 2 cm. The fruit bodies are placed where the temperature is maintained at 5–8°C and the humidity is 75–80%. The condition encourages vigorous fruit body growth. When the stem becomes long about 2–3 cm from the mouth of the bottle, a thick-waxed paper or plastic film is rolled around the mouth to hold the fruit body upright (Fig. 13.1).

Harvesting

When the fruit bodies are about 13–14 cm long, the rolled paper is removed and the fruit bodies are pulled up from the bottle and

Fig. 13.1 ***Flammulina velutipes*** **Grown in Container.**

packed. It takes about 50–60 days from the initial fruiting to the crop. The same bottles can be raised to obtain a second crop, but the quantity of fruit bodies is less and the quality also declines with the time. The first crop usually amounts to 100–140 g/800 ml bottle and the second crop 60–80 g in the same bottle. The cultivation of *F. velutipes* needs more improvement.

Chapter 14

Cultivation of *Pholiota nameko*

Nameko was a common name applied to the different mushroom, with a viscid or glutinous pileus such as *Flammulina velutipes, Pholiota nameko, P. adiposa, P. lenta, P. lubirica* and Kuehneromyces.

Pholiota nameko (T. Ito) S. Ito et. Imai, "nameko" is one of the four important wood inhabiting cultivated mushrooms found in Japan together with *Lentinus edodes, Flammulina velutipes* and *Pleurotus ostreatus.* Compared with other mushrooms, it is medium in size. From its glutinous substance it derives its name "nameko", which means viscid mushroom. Because of its good flavour and glutinous viscosity, it is generally used in Japanese dishes such as miso soup, cooked fresh with grated radish and steamed in a pipkin.

The "nameko" grows on dead trunks or stumps of deciduous trees, especially *Fagus crenata, F. japonica* and *Quercus magnolica* var. *grosseserrata.* That is why this fungus is naturally collected from Japan, there in rainy season mostly the fruit bodies are seen under natural conditions.

The maximum, minimal and optimum temperature is 32°C, below 8°C and 24–26°C respectively. In "nameko" cultures, the moisture content of the substrate (sawdust, rice bran beds and bed logs) is much more important at the time of mycelial growth than the aerial or soil moisture. When the moisture content of the sawdust, rice bran medium is within the range of 333–94% (on dry basis), mycelial growth will increase with increased moisture content. However, 150–160% is the most favourable condition for cultivation. Nameko mycelium can grow on the log woods of *Fagus crenata* and *Aesculus tubinata* immediately after felling, even though, this is normally not the best condition for growth.

The temperature range for fruiting in most of the cultivated mushrooms is generally lower than that for mycelial growth. The temperature needed for fruiting in "nameko", Arita (1964b) tested 45 stocks and divided his results into two groups in high temperature group i.e., 20–8°C and (2) low temperature group 15–5°C and found temperature fluctuation is not necessary for primordia initiation.

Temperature also affects the growth of fruit bodies. If the temperature is high (above 15°C), the pileus will be small and the stipe will be slender. On the contrary, under low temperature conditions (below 8°C), the pileus opens late and the fruit bodies become larger.

Under natural climatic conditions in Japan, the stocks of the high temperature type, produce fruit bodies from June to July and September to November and the low temperature stocks develop fruit bodies from October to December under suitable rainfall.

Moisture, light and aeration

Nameko is one of the hygrophilous fungus and needs high moisture for fruiting as compared to other cultivated mushrooms such as *L. edodes, F. velutipes* and *P. ostreatus.* According to bed log field survey in Japan, rain conditions play an important role in fruiting time and yield of "nameko". The number of rainy days corelates more closely to fruiting than the amount of precipitation. If "nameko" receives little rain for about one month previous to the fruiting sea-

Fig. 14.1. *Pholiota Nameko.*

son, almost no fruit body develops even though the temperature condition is favourable.

Light is absolutely necessary for fruiting. Morphological abnormalities, such as long slender stipe and thin rudimentary pilei, occur under dark or dim light. Although, no data on the effect of aeration have been obtained but it is known from experience that stagnant humid air or a CO_2 laden atmosphere inhibit the development of pileus and cause other morphological abnormalities. In order to maintain a normal transpiration rate from fruit bodies as well as substrates (sawdust and bed logs), an adequate supply of fresh air with suitable humidity is necessary, this favours primordia initiation and fruit body development.

Mycelial growth and mushroom production of "nameko" are generally related to the kind of sawdust and log woods used. The addition of a suitable amount of rice bran to sawdust compost increases the yield of fruit bodies and the amount of rice bran needed, varies according to different tree spp. Generally suitable amounts of rice bran added are 5–10% (dry wt. basis) for the sawdust of broad-leaved trees and 10–15% for the conifers.

In India, the cultivation of *Pholiota* spp. was reported by Krishna and Sharma (1989). They tried its cultivation on rice straw and sawdust and they found sawdust better than rice straw. They used grain spawn and sawdust of Populus trees and amended with 10% rice bran and 0.5% calcium carbonate, moisture level 75% and mixture was filled in empty bottle and autoclaved. After autoclaving the bottles were inoculated and incubated at 25°C.

Cultivation

Sawdust with 10% rice bran and 0.5% calcium carbonate was steamed for 60 min. in a container covered with polypropylene sheets. The temperature was lowered down to 25°C and polypropylene sheet was removed aseptically. Sawdust was inoculated with 2% sawdust spawn or grain spawn and the polypropylene sheet was again wrapped. The spawned bottles or boxes were incubated at 25°C.

Cropping

After complete spawn run, the top polypropylene sheet was removed from the bottle or boxes, the temperature was brought down to 15–20°C and relative humidity 90–95% by a faint drizzling rain. The fruit bodies appeared after 20 days, four to five flushes were harvested within 90 days (Fig. 14.1).

Chapter 15

Cultivation of *Shiitake* (*Lentinus edodes*)

Lentinus edodes known as Shiang-gu in China and *Shiitake* in Japan, is the second most important edible mushroom in the world from product point of view and is most popular cultivated mushroom in Japan, China and other far eastern countries. For a long time, this mushroom has been valued for its unique taste and flavour.

A famous Chinese doctor Wu Shui, during Ming dynasty (1368–1644) wrote that the *Lentinus* mushroom was capable of generating stamina, curing cold, improving the blood circulation and lowering blood pressure. It is now proved that *Lentinus* contains compounds that reduce the serum cholestrol level in human, which in turn, improves the patient in respect to hypertension. Recent medical experiments have shown that *Shiitake* stimulates the immune system which acts against cancer cells. *Shiitake* has also been found to have antiviral activity.

Lentinus edodes is estimated to be cultivated for the first time between 1000–1100. Ito (1978) stated that cultivation began in China about 800 years ago and primitive form of cultivation was introduced to Japan by Chinese farmers and towards the end of 17th century or beginning of 18th century (275–300 years ago), semi-cultivation technique developed by Japanese. Now the Japanese have improved and modified the methods to such an extent that Japan today leads in production, producing over two-thirds of *Shiitake* grown in the world during 1983–84.

At present, there is an increased interest in *Lentinus* cultivation in other countires of the world particularly in Europe and America as well as in Asia. The interest has been inspired by the success of Japanese growers whose techniques are now being initiated and modified. It has become a source of subsidiary income for many farmers in Japan. *Shiitake* mushroom is on top of Agricultural and forestry export of Japan.

Japanese method

The most suitable wood is oak. Pure culture spawn are impregnated in sawdust or for greater efficiency of inoculation, in small wedge-shaped piece of wood called "Tanegoma". The logs are planted with these spawn in spring and after the mycelium has grown through the wood, fruit bodies of *Shiitake* begin to grow out on the logs. With this method steady production is obtained.

Spawn

The pure culture spawn is prepared by mixing rice bran with sawdust, autoclaved and inoculated with mycelium and kept at temperature 24–28°C. The spawn is prepared on autoclaved wedge shaped, round wedge shaped or rod shaped pieces of wood of various spp. of oak. Rod-shaped pieces are usually about 1.5 cm in diameter and 2.0 cm in length.

Felling and cross cutting of trees for cultivation: Trees for cultivation are felled in autumn. If the cut is made at the wrong time, the bark strip off easily and chances of contamination of wood fungi increases before the establishment of *Shiitake* mycelium. *Shiitake* mycelium has to face more competition with the wild fungus, as it is grown in open, near the forest and no pasteurization of the substrate is done.

The another most important point is determination of time of cutting, as sugar content of the wood (in oak) begins to increase considerably, when about one-third of leaves have turned red in autumn and continues to increase, until just before budding in spring. The mycelium of *Shiitake* will get high per cent of carbohydrate which will help to spread the mycelium fast.

After trees are felled, the trunks remain in the forest and just before inoculation time they are cut into logs about 1 m long and 5–15 cm in diameter. The thicker branches are also used.

Inoculation

The growers who use solid pieces of inoculum, drill or pound into the log holes, which corresponds in size to the desired size of the inoculum. In case of sawdust spawn, the incisions or holes are more or less of the same size as used with the chip spawn. The holes and incisions are painted with hot wax in order to prevent evaporations. The number of holes or incisions is calculated to correspond about 15–20 holes per log.

Laying

After inoculation, the "bed logs" are placed in a position favourable for the development of the mycelium. This is done on the site which is especially selected for this "laying operation". The site is called "Laying yard".

The area where the air is extremely dry in spring, the pre-laying has been generally used. The siding or standing "bed logs" are generally used. The siding or standing bed logs are placed in the same spot. The piles of bed logs are covered with straw mat or Vinyl mat or any other material in order to keep out the extremely dry air. Pre-laying continues until the rainy season.

The laying yard should never be kept excessively moist, because of the danger of contamination of logs with more competing wood destroyer. If the laying takes place during the rainy season, very little watering will be necessary, but during dry season, the logs should be watered lightly. The optimum temperature for development of the mycelium of *Shiitake* is between 24–28°C.

In the laying yard, the bed logs are put in an obliquely upright position at a small angle to the surface of the earth with the single logs laid crosswise to increase aeration (Fig. 15.1).

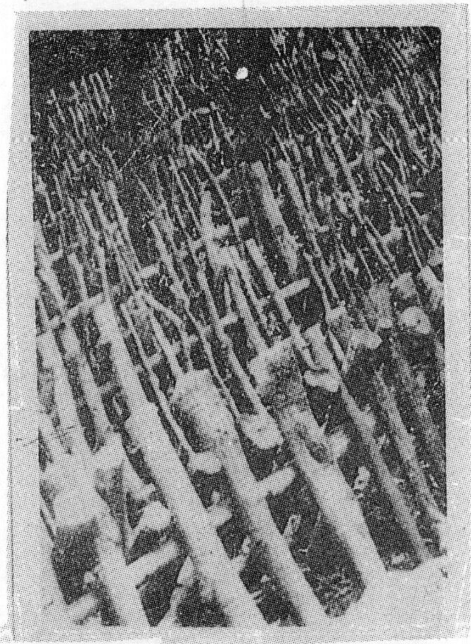

Fig. 15.1. Bed Logs in Laying Yard.

Raising

After the mycelium has permeated thoroughly in the wood which may happen any time after one or usually a year and a half after inoculation depending on the kind of wood, spawn, weather and laying yard condition and *Shiitake* strains. The logs are transferred to other place called "Raising yard". For fruiting, the temperature should be between 12–20°C. The fruiting of *Shiitake* requires considerably more moisture than the vegetative growth. The raising yard must be better shaded and the moisture must be constantly high. In the raising yard, the logs are placed more upright leaning in rows against parallel lines of bamboo fences. Usually transfer of logs should take place during winter, so that they will be ready for cropping in early spring.

Cropping

The fruit bodies of *Shiitake* grow in spring and fall. The spring crop as a rule is more abundant and fruit bodies are often of better quality and are more suitable for drying. Usually in spring crop, once the logs begin to produce, they will continue to do so for 3–6 years (Fig. 15.2).

Fig. 15.2. Lentinus Edodes Growing on Logs.

The producing logs are kept wet by watering. No other care is necessary except daily harvesting. The fruit body at the picking stage should be young, just at the time, when they begin to sporulate with a still strongly convex pileus and traces of veils are visible.

Taiwan method of cultivation

There are not many *Fagaceas* mainly oak trees are grown in Taiwan. It used to take lot of time to find suitable species and size of wood for *Shiitake* culture. In Taiwan the bag method of cultivation was developed which became very popular and is commercially used. Following are the stages in bag method of cultivation:

Stage 1—*Construction of plastic mushroom growing houses*

Temperature, humidity and ventilation are the main factors which should be controlled. For controlling these factors, economically constructed house of bamboo was made. It is lined inside with polyethylene film about 0.4 mm thick. Rice straw is put on the roof of the plastic house in order to prevent strong sun radiation and heat penetration. Normally the plastic is rollable on both sides of the house. At the time of high temperature the side film can be rolled up in order to help hot air out.

Stage 2—*Preparation of sawdust medium*

The medium for growing *Shiitake* in the plastic bag is sawdust with 5–10% of the rice bran to enrich the medium. Sometimes calcium carbonate is added to adjust pH of the medium.

Sawdust is stacked outdoor for 5–10 days, mixed with rice bran at proper ratio and is adjusted to a measurable water content. The process is the same as that of sawdust spawn medium.

Stage 3—*Bagging and sterilization of medium*

The plastic bag is about 15–18 cm in length and 10–12 cm in diameter. A special designed plastic ring is wrapped at the top end of the bag to form a bottleneck with a cotton plug in it. These growing bags can be prepared by the growers themselves.

The mixed sawdust are packed in plastic bags and pressed to form a cylindrical cake. They are sterilized in a special steaming room, autoclaved at 90–100°C for 4 hours.

Stage 4—*Inoculation and incubation*

The bags are then inoculated and transferred to a growing house maintained at 28°C or lower. The inoculation process is like that of the normal spawn making, which is operated by two workers in an aseptic conditioned room. They just remove the cotton plug for spawn inoculation. The spawn is prepared ahead of time for inoculation.

The selection of strain for bag cultivation should be done carefully. Normally temperature sensitive strain is used in this method.

The spread of mycelium in the bag will take place in about 25–30 days if the room temperature is maintained. But at that time it is still early for fruiting, wait for 40–50 days until the surface of the bagged sawdust becomes dark brown in colour and hard textured.

Stage 5—*Fruiting*

At the fruiting, the top end of the bag is cut off and turned to moistened soil floor in growing room.

After 2–3 days of moistened treatment, the bagged sawdust mixture is placed in original top side up condition. This process is similar to the laying and raising process in the traditional wood log cultivation method.

Stage 6—*Cropping*

Normally watering is not necessary at the cropping stage, except when air is too dry.

Once the bagged sawdust mixture begin to fruit they will continue to do so for 5 months. The fruit bodies should be young at picking, just before the time when they begin to sporulate.

The harvesting period of the bag cultivation is shorter than the log cultivation. There are usually only three to four flushes in a crop and the yield of each bag is about 300–400 g. After the cropping period, the bags are removed from the room. Growing house should be cleaned for next cropping.

Kalberer (1989) used the substrate having conifers sawdust, wheat bran, calcium carbonate and water. He preferred heat treatment than autoclaving the substrate. Before heat treatment, the moisture content of the substrate was adjusted to 70% of its weight. The dry matter of the substrate – 30% the substrate weight, consisted of 75–85% sawdust dry matter and of 15–30% of wheat bran. The calcium carbonate is about 1% of the dry matter. After thorough mixing of sawdust, wheat bran and calcium carbonate, tap water was added and mixing was repeated. Heat treatment he gave was 95°C for 24 hrs in an oven or room without fresh air supply.

The substrate was filled in 5 L. pots. Pots with an increasing diameter from bottom to top is best suited. The substrate blocks in this 5 L. glass pots had a diameter of 18–20 cm, a height of 20–25 cm and a weight of 2.5–3.0 kg. The substrate is pressed gently.

Excessive pressing makes it difficult to spawn the substrate after heat treatment. The pots were covered with aluminium foil and were kept at 95°C for 24 hrs. in an oven or room without fresh air. A room with humidity control is preferred for heat treatment. Weight loss due to evaporation during the heat treatment was about 100 g for a block of 2500 g.

Before spawning, the substrate was allowed to cool down to room temperature, 4% grain spawn was used. To spawn the substrate, aluminium foil was removed for a short time and the spawn was poured from the container directly on to the surface of the substrate. A heat treated sterile metal rod was used to punch 4–6 holes all the way down to the bottom of the substrate. Grain spawn was filled in these holes using the rods. Immediately, after spawning the container was closed with aluminium foil. The spawned substrate was incubated for spawn run at 25°C for 1–2 month in a dark room without humidity and fresh air supply. Block of 2500 g, lost 40–90 g during the incubation period. Author preferred two months incubation, because a substrate with a denser mycelium gives a stronger flush and the surface of the substrate is less vulnerable to infection.

During the incubation period the mycelium of *L. edodes* densely penetrate the substrate. On the surface of the substrate, the mycelium was very dense and fluffy, where it touched the aluminium foil it corroded it. Polythene sheet had to be used to cover the holes in the bottom of the pot.

At the end of the incubation period substrates were removed from the pot. The blocks were incubated in the harvesting room at 17–19°C and very high relative humidity of 95–99%. Depending on the position of the block in the spawning room, they were exposed to 20–150 hrs. In this range, there is no difference in yield or quality of the harvested sporophore.

After a good flush of fruit bodies, the blocks were markedly lighter. To get the high yield in short time, a high moisture content of the mixture is very important. The light blocks have to be soaked in water. Before soaking, the dense mycelial layer on the surface of the blocks had to be punctured.

Different workers have given different formulae for bag cultivation method:

Mori *et al.* (1974)

Sawdust (*Quercus crispula*)	80%
Rice bran	20%
Water content adjusted to	65%

Ham *et al.* (1981)

Hard wood sawdust	89.8%
Rice bran	10.0%
$CaCO_3$	0.2%
Water content adjusted to	60.0%

Song (1986)

Hard wood sawdust	100 kg
Rice bran	8–16 kg
Corn powder or millet or rice	4–8 kg
$CaCO_3$	0.6–1 kg
Water	59–65%
	(180 kg)

Royse *et al.* (1981)

Mixed hard wood sawdust	80.0%
White millet	10.0%
Wheat bran	10.0%
Water	4 litres

Difference between bag method and log method of cultivation:

1. Bag cultivated *Shiitake* can grow in sawdust, while wood log *Shiitake* largely depends on limited species of wood.
2. Bag cultivation can be adjusted in size of bags in order to standardize, while wood log cultivation depends on size (diameter of the natural timber).
3. Bag cultivation is easier for mechanization, while log cultivation is difficult.
4. Bag method of cultivation is easier, if the weight of the bag is adjusted around 1 kg/bag.
5. The harvesting period of the bag cultivation is shorter than the log cultivation. There are only three to four flushes in a crop.

Important factors:

1. Various additives may be added to the sawdust to encourage mycelial growth, the most common being rice bran and corn meal.
2. The pH should be adjusted to 5.5–7.0 using calcium carbonate or sodium carbonate.
3. The correct water content of the mixture is of paramount importance and is often determined by squeezing the mixture in the hand after which the sawdust should hold together.

4. The quality of material used in manufacturing of bag is important as some may produce inhibitory substance, which may prevent mycelial growth, especially during autoclaving.
5. Sterilization of bag is done either by steaming or autoclaving.
6. The quality and purity of the sawdust must be ensured, as chemicals used as preservative on the wood or wood impregnated with salt water will inhibit mycelial development.
7. During mycelium development, bag should be kept in condition of low light intensity and high humidity with little ventilation.
8. When mycelial development is complete, the tops of the bags are removed and vigorous watering is applied as fine mist by overhead spray to induce fruiting.
9. Immediately after watering, the bags are inverted and water is taken up from the floor by capillary action.
10. The bags are left inverted overnight then turned upright again The procedure may be repeated up to three times. Coincidental with watering, light intensity and ventilation should be increased.
11. One should be sure whether the strain in suitable for log or bag method of cultivation.
12. *Shiitake* mycelium grows more rapidly in the dark but some light is necessary during mycelial growth for the development of mushrooms. Later, 10–50 lux should be the light intensity for future development of fruiting and usually 8–12 hrs/day depending on the strain used.

Chapter 16

Delicious Recipes of Mushroom

Mushroom omelette

Eggs	2
Small mushrooms	3
Butter	25 g

Chop mushrooms and place them in a pan. Add butter, a little salt and pepper and simmer the mushrooms. Make up and fry the omelette mixture and when ready, add the simmered mushrooms, fold over and cook for another few seconds, then serve piping hot.

Stuffed potatoes

Finely chopped mushrooms	500 g
Finely chopped onions	120 g
Fresh lime juice	3 teaspoons
Butter	125 g
Grated cheese	12.5 g
Salt	according to taste

Melt butter in pan. Add mushrooms and onions and fry them lightly. Now stir in the lime juice and salt. Cook till the water is dried. Take medium size potatoes, boil a little so that they are soft from outside. Peel off the skin, scoop out and stuff the hollow potatoes with the mushroom preparation. Place the potatoes upright on an oven dish. Put a little fat over them and place in pre-heated oven. Allow them to cook until well browned. Serve with cooked tomatoes.

Mushrooms on toast

Cup-mushrooms	2 to 3 large ones
Butter	30 g

Take two to three large cup-mushrooms with their gills showing an attractive deep pink colour. Remove the stem and mince with a little parsley and a small onion (optional). Add salt and pepper and cook in butter or ghee. Beat up an egg, add a pinch of bread crumbs and stir into the simmering mushroom stalks. As soon as the mixture is thickened, place the mushroom caps and bake for four to five minutes and serve on cripss hot toasts.

Mushroom soup

Fresh mushrooms	500 g
Butter	50 g
White flour (*maida*)	2 tablespoons full
Salt	to taste
Ground spices (cardamom, red chillies, cinnamom and pepper)	4 g
Milk	1 litre

Clean and chop the fresh mushrooms. Melt butter in a pan and saute the mushrooms in it. Add small and let the mixture boil for five to seven minutes. Dissolve maida in little cold water and add to the boiling milk and mushroom mixture to thicken it. Give two boils and add salt and spices. Serve hot.

Mushroom pakoras

Medium sized mushrooms (without stem)	6
Egg	1
Gram flour (*besan*)	10 g
Baking powder	a pinch
Salt and red pepper	according to taste
Fine white bread crumbs, Oil to fry	sufficient

Beat the egg and add flour, baking powder, salt and red pepper and make a batter. Add little water if needed. Dip mushrooms in a batter and roll in bread crumbs. Heat the oil and fry few mushrooms pakoras at a time, till they become brown.

Mushroom pulao

Mushrooms	250 g
Rice	100 g
Onion	1 small
Cumin seeds	½ tablespoon
Cardamom	1
Bay leaf	2

Cloves	1–2
Black pepper	2–3
Ghee (cooking fat)	2 tablespoons
Salt	according to taste

Wash mushrooms, cut and chop lengthwise. Clean and soak the rice for 10 minutes. Heat ghee and fry mushrooms lightly. Keep them aside. In the same ghee add cumin, cardamom, cloves, black pepper and bay leaves. When cumin seeds begin to crackle add onion. Brown them lightly. Add rice and double the quantity of water and salt to taste. After rice begins to boil, add mushrooms to the rice. Cook on a slow fire, till the pulao is ready.

Mushroom pickle (1)

Fresh mushrooms	500 g
Salt	20 g
Ginger (ground)	5 g
Onion (chopped)	20 g
Mace (ground)	2 g
Fenugreek (*Methi* seeds) (ground coarsely)	10 g
White pepper (powdered)	20 g
Red chillies	10 g
Glacial acetic acid (conc. vinegar)	10 g
Rape seed oil	100 g

Use button mushrooms. Immerse them in cold water for a few minutes and drain. Put clean mushrooms in a pan and mix with salt, pepper, mace, fenugreek, red chillies. Fry onion and ginger in oil to a light brown colour and mix with mushrooms. Add vinegar and cook for 10 minutes. Pour the whole mixture into small glass jars, taking care that all the spices are divided equally in the jars. Leave it for a few days.

Mushroom pickle (2)

Mushrooms	250 g
Onion	50 g
Ginger	1 inch piece
Garlic	2–3 cloves
Mustard oil	100 g
Salt	1 teaspoon full heaped
Red chilli powder	½ teaspoon full
Garam masala	½ teaspoon full

Gur	100 g
Vinegar	¾ cup
Mustard seeds	10 g (coarsely ground)

Wash mushrooms, cut the larger mushroom lengthwise and leave the smaller mushroom uncut. Heat oil in a pan and fry the mushrooms lightly. Take them out and in the same oil fry chopped onion, ginger and garlic to golden brown. Side by side dissolve gur in vinegar in a separate pan. Mix the mushroom and gur syrup with the fried onion, ginger and garlic. Take the pan off the fire. Bottle the pickle.

Mushrooms and peas

Mushrooms	200 g
Peas	200 g
Onion	1 small
Tomato	1 medium size
Ghee	1 tablespoon full
Cumin	½ tablespoon full
Garam masala	1/4 tablespoon full
Salt	to taste
Green chillies	1

Wash mushrooms and cut into two pieces lengthwise. Shell the peas. Put ghee on the fire, add cumin seeds to it. When they crackle add onions, tomatoes, mushrooms, shelled peas, salt and half teaspoon of turmeric powder. Let the mixture cook on a slow fire. When water dried up and peas are cooked, remove from the fire. Add garam masala to it.

Variation

Before removing from the fire add a little cream, if cream is not available, add two tablespoons full of corn flour paste, which was prepared in water.

Mushrooms and paneer

Mushrooms	500 g
Paneer	250 g
Onion	100 g
Tomatoes	100 g
Ghee	2 tablespoon full
Salt	to taste
Garam masala	1 teaspoon full

Wash mushrooms and cut into two halves lengthwise. Dice paneer into 2" cubes. Chop onions and cut tomatoes into small pieces. Heat ghee in a pan, put chopped onion in it and let it brown, add tomatoes to it. Simmer it for 5 minutes. Add mushroom, paneer and salt. Cook at slow fire till water of mushroom dries up. Add garam masala and serve hot.

Mushroom samosa

For stuffing:

Mushroom	200 g
Onion (chopped)	1 big or 2 small
Green chillies (chopped)	1 tablespoon full
Coriander leaves (chopped)	1 tablespoon full
Salt	to taste

For covering :

White flour (Maida)	250 g
Ghee	3 desert spoon
Salt	½ tea spoon

Cut mushroom in small pieces, chop onion. Heat ghee in a pan and add mushroom, chopped onion, green chillies and salt. Put on fire, when water dries up, add coriander leaves. Use this for stuffing.

Sieve white flour, put ghee and make a soft dough by adding water. Make small balls with dough and role them into small chapaties. Cut each into two halves and take one part of it. Fill the samosa with the stuffing. Heat ghee and deep fry. Serve hot with tomato sauce or green chutney.

Liver with mushroom

Mushroom	200 g
Liver	100 g
Garlic (paste)	4 cloves
Tomato (cut into small pieces)	1 big
Onion	1 big or 2 small
Ginger (paste)	1 teaspoon
Salt and red chillies	to taste

Grind onion and keep it on fire till brown with little ghee in a pan. Add garlic-ginger paste and small pieces of tomato. Put salt and red chillies. Fry for 2–3 minutes. Cook liver pieces in the cooked masala till soft. Add mushroom to it and cook till water dries up. It is ready to be served at lunch or dinner time.

References

Agarwala, R.K., 1973, How to grow mushroom ? *Indian J. Mushroom* **1**(1): 17–21.

Alexopoulos, C.J., 1962, *Introductory Mycology,* Wiley Eastern Pvt. Ltd., p. 613.

Alicbusan, R.V., 1979, Mushroom production technology for rural development, *In: Food and Nutrition Bulletin Supplementary,* 2nd November, 1979, pp. 99–104.

Anderson, E.E. and C.R. Fellers, 1942, The food value of mushrooms (*A. campestris*), *Proc. Amer. Soc. Hort. Sci.* **41**: 301.

Arita, I., 1964, Nameko culture Kinjin (Tottori Mycol. Inst.) 110, 44–56 (in Jpn).

Asthana, R.P., 1947, Mushroom cultivation in Central Provinces, *Mag. Agr. Coll. Nagpur,* **32**: 25–31.

Atkins, F.C., 1972, *Mushroom Growing Today,* Faber and Faber Ltd., London, p. 188.

Atkinson, C.F., 1961, *Studies of American Fungi Mushrooms Edible, Poisonous,* Hafner Pub. Co., New York, pp. 322.

Bahl, Nita, 1982, Polybag method—a new technique for cultivation of paddy straw mushroom (*Volvariella volvacea*), *Indian Phytopath.* **36**: 702–704.

Bahl, Nita and P.N. Chowdhry, 1981, *Podospora faurelii*—a new competitor in the mushroom (*Volvariella volvacea*), *Curr. Sci.* **50**: 378.

Bahl, Nita, S. Ghai and D. Prasad, 1981, Pests problems of button mushroom (*Agaricus bisporus*), Third International Symposium on Plant Pathology, Division of Mycology and Plant Pathology, Indian Agricultural Research Institute, New Delhi-110012. (Abstract pp. 209.)

Baker, J.D. and J.W. Baker, 1981, Barrel composting, *Mush Sci.* **11**: 201–210.

Bano, Zakia, 1976, The nutritive value of mushrooms, *Indian Mush. Sci.* **1**: 473–487.

Bano, Z. and H.C. Srivastava, 1962, Studies in the cultivation of

Pleurotus sp. on paddy straw, *Food Sci.* **12**: 363–365.

Bano, Z. and M.V. Patwardhan, 1979, Post harvest handling and processing of mushrooms, National Seminar on Research Production, Processing and Marketing of Mushrooms, I.C.A.R.

Bano, Z., S. Rajarathnam and N. Nagaraja, 1979, Some aspects on the cultivation of *Pleurotus flabellatus* in India, *Mush. Sci.* **10**(2): 567–608.

Bano, Z., K.S. Srinivasan and H.C. Srivastava, 1963, Amino acid composition of the protein from a mushroom (*Pleurotus flabellatus*), *Appl. Microbiol.* **11**: 184–187.

Block, S.S., 1965, Garbage composting for mushroom production, *Appl. Microbiol.* **13**: 5–9.

Block, S.S. and S.H. Rao, 1962, Sawdust composting for mushroom production, *Mush. Sci.* **5**: 104.

Bohus, G., 1959, Investigation concerning the life process of the cultivated mushroom, *Mush. Sci.* **4**: 86–131.

Bose, S.R., 1921, Possibilities of mushroom industry in India by cultivation, *Agric. J. India* **16**: 643–647.

Bose, S.R. and A.B. Bose 1940, An account of edible mushrooms of India, *Sci. Cult.* **6**: 141–149.

Callow, E., 1831, 'Fellows', London.

Chakravarty D.K. and B.Sarkar, 1978, Cultivation of *Pleurotus sajor-caju* in West Bengal, *Indian Agric.* **22**: 213–222.

Chang, S.T., 1978, *Volvariella volvacea, The Biology and Cultivation of Edible Mushrooms,* Academic Press, New York, San Francisco, London, 1978.

Chang, S.T., 1987, World production of cultivated edible mushroom in 1986. *Mush. Jour. for the Tropics* **7**: 117–120.

Cheng, S., and C.C. Tu, 1978, *Auricularia* spp. In: *the Biology and cultivation of Edible mushroom.* (S.T. Chang and W.A. Hayes eds.) pp. 605–25. New York Academic Press.

Chowdhry, P.N. and Nita Bahl. 1980, Notes on *Conidiobolus coronata and Dactylaria thaumasia from* India, *Indian Phytopath.* **33**: 611–613.

Chua, S.E. and S.Y. Ho, 1973, Fruiting on sterile agar and cultivation of straw mushroom (*Volvariella* sp) on paddy straw, banana leaves and sawdust, *World Crops.* **25**: 90–91.

Cooke, R.C., 1977, Fungi, Man and His Environment, Largmann, London and New York, pp 144.

Dang, R.L. and R.P. Singh, 1978, Preservation of mushrooms, *Indian Mush. Sci.* **1**: 215–224.

Derikx, P.J.L., H.J.M Op den Camp, C. van der Drift, L.J.LD. van Griensven and G.D. Vogels 1990. Biomass and biological activity during the production of compost used as a substrate in mushroom cultivation. *Applied and Environmental Microbiology* **56**: 3029–3039.

Dhar, B.L. 1995. Mushroom Farm design In: Advances in Horticulture vol 13-Mushroom (Eds) K.L. Chadha and S.K. Sharma, Malhotra Publishing House, New Delhi pp. 597–619.

Duggar, B.M. 1905, Some principles in mushroom growing and spawn making. *U.S. Dept. Agr. Tech., Bull.* **85**: 1–60.

Edwards, R.L., 1949, MRA Report on synthetic compost, *Mush. Grow. Ass. Bull.* **15**: 84–88.

Edwards, R.L., 1950, Directions for making MRA compost, *Mushroom* Res. Station, Yaxley, Peterborough, England, 'Ann. Report', 1949, 45–48.

Edwards, R.L., 1975, Ninth International Mushroom Science Congress *Mushroom Journal* 1975, January.

Edwards, R.L. and P.B. Flegg, 1953, Experiments with artifical mixtures for casing mushroom beds, *Mush. Sci.* **2**: 143–160.

Eger, G., 1962, Untersucherngen Zur Fruchtkorper Bildung Des Kulturchampignens, *Mush. Sci.* **5**: 314–320.

Evered, C.E., R. Noble and P.T. Atkey 1995. Microbial populations and straw degradation in mushroom compost prepared in controlled environments. *Mush. Sci.* **14**: 245–255.

Flegg, P.B., 1953, Pore space and related properties of casing materials, *Mush. Sci.* **2**: 149–160.

Flegg, P.B., 1959, The function of the compost and casing layer in relation to fruiting and growth of the cultivated mushroom, *Mush. Sci.* **4**: 205–210.

Flegg, P.B., S. Jutle and J.B. Rothwell, 1966, Methods and rates of spawning mushroom beds, *Expt. Hort.* **12**: 32–35.

Fletcher, J.T., P.F. White, and R.H. Gaze, 1986, Mushrooms: Pest and Disease Control. Intercept. Ponteland, Newcastle upon Tyne. pp. 156.

Gandy, D.G., 1960, Watery stipe of cultivated mushrooms, *Nature, Lond.* **185**: 482–483.

Gandy, D.G. and M. Hollings, 1962, Die back of mushrooms: a disease associated with a virus, *Ann. Rep. Glass House Crops. Res. Inst. 1961:* 103–108.

Garcha, H.S., 1980, Mushroom growing, Punjab Agricultural University, Ludhiana.

Gerrits, J.P.G., 1974, Development of a synthetic compost for mushroom growing based on wheat straw and chicken manure, *Netherland J. Agri, Sci.* **22**: 175–194.

Gerrits, J.P.G. 1987 Bied composteren in tunnels perspectif. *De champignoncultur* **31**: 357–365.

Gerrits, J.P.G. and L.J.L.D. van Griensven 1990, New Developments in Indoor Composting (tunnel process). *Mush J.* **205**: 21–29.

Gerrits, J.P.G., H.C. Bells-Koning and F.M. Muller, 1965. Changes in compost constituents during composting pasteurisation and cropping, *Mush. Sci.* **6**: 225–243.

Gormley, T.R. and C. Mac Canna, 1967, *Irish. J. Agric. Res.* **6**(2): 255.

Gulliver, A., F.C. Miller, E. Harper and B.J. Macauley 1991. Environmentally controlled composting a commercial scale in Australia. *Mush. Sci.* **13**: 155–164.

Gupta, G.K., B.S. Bajaj and D. Suryanarayana, 1970, Studies on the cultivation of paddy straw mushroom, (*V. volvacea and V. diplasia*), *Indian Phytopath.* **23**: 615–620.

Han. Y.H., W.T. Ueng, L.C. Chen and S. Cheng, 1981, Physiology and Ecology of *Lentinus edodes* (Berk) Sing. *Mush. Sci.* **11**(2): 623–658.

Harper, E.F., C. Miller and B.J. Macauley. 1992. Physical management and interpretation of an environmentally controlled composting ecosystem. *Aust. J. Exp. Agric.* **32**: 657–667.

Hayes, W.A., 1974, The casing layer-A review for the Aston Seminar on mushroom science, *The Mush. Jour. No.* 13:12–16.

Hayes, W.A. and N. Haddad, 1976, The food value of the cultivated mushroom and its importance to the mushroom industry, *The Mushroom J.,* **40**: 104–110.

Hayes, W.A. and P.N. Randle, 1969, Use of molassess as an ingredient wheat straw mixture used for the preparation of mushroom composts, *Rep. Glass House Crops. Res. Inst.* p. 142.

Heltay, I., 1959, Influence of storage at the temperature of 2°C below zero on productivity of the spawn, *Mush. Sci.* **4**: 362–32.

HO, M.S. 1989. A new technology "Plastic Bag cultivation method" for growing *Shiitake* mushroom. *Mush. Sci.* **12**(2): 303–309.

Hollings, M. and O.M. Stone, 1969, Viruses in fungi, Sci. Progr. (Oxford), **57**: 371.

Hollings, M. and O.M. Stone, 1971, Viruses that infect fungi, *Ann. Rev. Phytopathology* **9**: 93–118.

Hu, K.J. and N. Lin, 1972, Study on granular spawn, *Mush. Sci.* **8**: 275–283.

Hughes, D.H. 1962, Preliminary characterisation of the lipid constituents of the cultivated mushroom *Agaricus campestris, Mush Sci,* **5**: 540–546.

Hussey, N.W., 1972, Pests in perspective, *Mush. Sci.* **8**: 183–192.

Ito, T., 1978, Cultivation of Lentinus edodes-Biology and cultivation of edible mushroom (S.T. Chang and W.A. Hayes edt) pp. 461–473. New York Academic Press.

Jandaik, C.L. 1995 Economics of Mushroom Cultivation. Advances in Horticulture Vol. 13. Mushroom (1995) Eds. K.L. Chadha and S.R. Sharma. Malhotra Publishing House.

Jandaik, C.L. and J.N. Kapoor, 1974, Artificial cultivation of *Pleurotus sajor caju* (Fr.) Singer, *The Mushroom J.* **22**: 405.

Jandiak, C.L. and J.N. Kapoor, 1974, Artificial cultivation of *Pluerotus sajor caju* Singer (Abst.) 1st Workshop on mushroom Res., Solan, H.P.

Kalberer, P.P. 1989, The cultivation of *Shiitake (Lentinus edodes)* on supplemented saw dust. *Mush. Sci.* **12**(2): 317–325.

Kannaiyan, S., 1974c, Edible mushrooms II. Cultivation of *Volvariella diplasia, Farm Fac.,* Feb.

Kannaiyan, S. and N.N. prasad, 1978 Production of paddy straw mushroom in India-A review, *Indian Mush. Sci.* **1**: 287–292.

Kapoor, J.N. and Nita Bahl, 1982, *Mushroom growing for beginners,* Division of Mycology and Plant Pathology, Indian Agricultural Research Insttute, New Delhi.

Kapoor, J.N. and Nita Bahl, 1983, Cultivation of button mushroom, *Gram Praudyogiki* **3**: 10–14.

Karosciene, S.C., 1969, Vitamin content of mushrooms, Thiamine and riboflavin content in fruit bodies of *Roziles caperata, Leit TSR Makslu Akad Darbeerser* **C**(2): 193–198.

Kaul, K.N., 1978, Prospects of large scale cultivation of paddy straw mushroom in Uttar Pradesh, *Indian Mush. Sci.* **1**: 305–310.

Kavaler, Lucy, 1967, Mushrooms, Moulds and Miracels, George G, Harrap and Co. Ltd., London, Toronto, Wellington, Sydney, p. 290.

Kezeli, T.A. and L.D. Dzabaridze, 1944, Bull. Acad. Sci. Georgian, SSA (cited by Gilbert and Robinson, 1957).

Kleermaeker, E.D., 1953, Some experiments on various casing sub. *Mush. Sci.* **2**: 139–142.

Kligman, A.M., 1950, *Mushroom Culture,* Kenneth Square, Pa. U.S.A., pp. 257.

Kneebone, L.K., J.D. Lockard and R.A. Hagar, 1962, Infectivity studies with X-disease, *Mush. Sci.* **5**: 461–467.

Krishna, A. and S.K. Sharma, 1989, Effect of various growth regulators on the mycelial yield of *Pholiota destruens* (Brond) gillet. *Mush. Sci.* **12**(2): 469–477.

Krishnamohan, G. and R. Jeya Rajan, 1978, Hollow bed–a new method of doubling yield of paddy straw mushroom, *Indian Mushroom Science* **1**: 319–323.

Krishnamurthy, C.S. and D. Lalithakumari, 1968, How to grow mushrooms in your farm ? *Indian Horticulture* **13**: 9–11.

Kumar, S., P.K. Seth and R.L. Munjal, 1975, Studies on quantities of gypsum and calcium carbonate singly and in combination of spawn production of *Agaricus bisporus, Ind. J. Mush.* **1**(2): 27.

Laborde, J., G. Lanzi, R. Francesscutti and E. Giordani 1993 Indoor Composting: general principles and large scale development in Italy. In: Mushroom Biology and Mushroom Products, S.T. Chang, J.A. Buswell and S.W. Chiu (eds). The Chinese University Press, Hong Kong, pp. 93–114.

Lambert, E.B., 1929, Normal mushrooms from artificial manure, *Science* **70**: 126–128.

Lambert, E.B. and H. Humfield, 1939, Mushroom casing soil in relation to yield, *USDA Circ.,* **507**: 1–11.

Last, F.T., 1970, Mushroom cultivation-mystique or method ? The changing scene (Pt. 1), M.G.A. *Bulletin* June 1970, pp. 259–273.

Lemke, I., 1968, Beobachtungen bei der Kiihllagerung von Kornerbrut, *Mush. Sci.* **7**: 543–552.

Lintzel, W., 1941, The nutritional value of edible mushroom protein, *Biochem. Acta.* **308**: 413–419.

Lintzel, W., 1943, Ueber den Nahrwert des Eiweisse essbarer Pilze, *Chem. Ztg.* **67**: 33–34.

MacCanna, C., 1969, Nitrogen supplementation of composts, *Mush. Sci.* **7**: 295–306.

MacCanna, C. and T.R. Gormley, 1969, Quality assessment of mushrooms: Relationship between moisture loss, colour and toughness of harvested cultivated mushrooms, *Mush. Sci.* **7**: 485–492.

Madan, M. and R.L. Munjal, 1983, Cultivation of Pleurotus sajor caju, *Gram Pradyogiki* **3**: 14–17.

Madic, V.R. and E.F. Roldan, 1965. A preliminary test on the effect on mushroom production of straw rendered sterile with the fumigent Dow fume MC-2, *Araneta J. Agric.* **12**: 233–238.

Mantel, E.F.K., R.K. Agarwala, and P.K. Seth, 1972. A guide to mushroom cultivation unit, Directorate of Extension. Ministry of Agriculture, New Delhi.

McCanee, P.A. and E.M. Widdowson, 1969, H.M.S.O.

McConnel, J.E. and W.B. Esselen, 1947, Carbohydrates in cultivated mushrooms, *Food Res.* **12**: 118–121.

Miller, F.C. 1994 Conventional Composting System. In: *Agaricus Compost,* N.G. Nair (ed.), *Australian Mushroom Growers Association. 'Windsor' NSW Australia* pp. 1–18.

Miller, F.C. 1996. Composting of municipal solid waste and its components. In: Microbiology of solid Wastes, A.C. Palmisano and M.A. Barlaz (eds) C.R.C. Press, Roca Raton, Florida pp. 115–154.

Miller, F.C., E.R. Harper, B.J. Macauley and A. Gulliver, 1990. Composting based on moderately thermophilic aerobic conditions for the production of commercial growing compost, *Aus. J. Exp. Agric* **30**: 415–425.

Morgareidge, K. 1958, AMI reports.

Mori, K., S. Fukai, and A. Zennyozi, 1976, Hybridization of *Shiitake (Lentinus edodes)* between cultivated strain of Japan and wild strains grown in Taiwan and New Guinea. *Mushroom Science* **9**(1): 391–403.

Munjal., R.L., 1973, Production of quality spawn of *Agaricus biporus and Volvaiella spp. Ind. J. Mush.* **1**(1): 1–11.

Muthukrishnan, P., 1971, Studies on Volvariella diplasia (Berk. and Br.) Sacc. *M.Sc. thesis, Annamalai University, Tamil Nadu India,* p. 199.

Muthukrishnan, P. and N.N. Prasad, 1971b, Nematode infection on *Volvariella diplasia, International Symp. Plant Pathol.,* New Delhi (Abstr.).

Muthukrishnan, P. and N.N. Prasad, 1977, Occurrence of Collembola infestation on *Volvariella displasia. Annamalai Univ. Agric. Res. Anna.* **2**: 83–84.

Nair, N.G., 1972, Observations on virus disease of the cultivated mushroom, *Agaricus bisporus* in Australia, *Mush. Sci.* **8**: 155–170.

Noble, R. and R.H. Gaze 1994. Controlled environment composting for mushroom cultivation: substrates based on wheat and barley straw and deep litter poultry manure. Jour Agric. Sc. April Cambridge **123**: 71–79.

O'Donoghue, D.C., 1965, Relationship between some compost factors and their effects on the yield of *Agaricus, Mush. Sci.* **6**: 245–254.

Overstijns, A. 1994. Indoor Composting System In, *Agaricus Compost.* N.G. Tan (ed.) *Australia Mushroom Grower Association Windsor, NSW, Australia* pp. 127–150.

Padwick, G.W., 1941, Mushroom cultivation in India, *Indian Farming* **11**: 363–366.

Perrin, P. and R. Gaze 1987. Controlled environmental compositing in bulk chambers and in troughs *Mush.* Sc. **12**: 489–497.

Pizer, N.H., 1937, Investigations into the environment and nutrition of the cultivated mushroom *Psalliota campestris,* 1: Some properties of composts in relation to the growth of the mycelium, *J. Agric, Sci* **27**: 349–367.

Purkayastha, R.P. and Andrila Chandra,1976. Indian edible mushrooms, Firma KLM Pvt. Ltd., Calcutta, p. 106.

Ramakrishnan, K., D. Lalithakumari, N. Shanmughen and C.S. Krishnamurthy, 1968, A simple technique for increasing the yield of straw mushroom, *Volvariella diplasia,* Madras Agric J. **55**: 194–195.

Ramasamy, K, and T.K. Kandaswamy, 1978, Spawn composition and spawning methods on yield of straw mushroom, *Indian Mush, Sci.* **1**: 277–282.

Ramsbottom, J., 1953, Mushrooms and Toadstool, Collins, London.

Rasmussen, C.R., 1961, Comparative cropping experiments between top spawing, through/mixed spawning, shake-up spawning and super spawning, *MGA Bull.* **141**: 381–396.

Rasmussen, C.R., 1962, The 16 day 'Normal' + 75% inactive composting process, *Mush. Sci.* **5**: 91–102.

Rasmussen, C.R., 1965, Combination of sulphate of ammonia, calcium carbonate, superphosphate and gypsum and their infulence in outside composting and cropping yield, *Mush. Sci.* **6**: 307–327.

Rasmussen, C.R., 1965, In forum on mushroom cultivation, *Mush. Sci.* **6**: 545–551.

Rasmussen, C.R., 1970, *MGA* Conference papers.

Rempe, H., Some experiments with sawdust compsot, *Mush. Sci.* **2**: 131–133.

Rolfe, R.T. and F.W. Rolfe, 1966. *The Romance of the Fungus World,* Johnson Reprint Corporation, New York, Johnson Reprint Co. Ltd., London, p. 309.

Ross, R.C. and P.J. Harris, 1983. The significance of thermophilic fungi in mushroom compost preparation. Scientia Horticultuerae **27**: 61–70.

Roy, M.K. and Nita Bahl, 1984, Gamma radiation for preservation of *Agaricus bisporus, Mushroom Journal* **136**: 124.

Royse, D.J., L.C. Schisler and D.A. Diohle, 1985, *Shiitake* mushrooms consumption, production and cultivation, *Interdescip Sci. Rev.* **10**: 329–335.

San Antonio, J.P. and S.W. Hwang, 1970, Liquid nitrogen preservation of spawn stocks of the cultivated *Agaricus bisporus (Lange), Sing. J. Am. Soc. Hort. Sci.* **95**: 656–659.

San Antonio, J.P. and S.W. Hwang, 1971, A method for the safe deposit of mushroom spawn stock cultures, *Mushroom News,* **19**: 10–12.

Shandilya, T.R., P.K. Seth, S. Kumar and R.L. Munjal, 1974, Effect of different spawning methods on the productivity of *Agaricus bisporus, Indian J. Mycol. Plant Pathol.,* **4**: 129–131.

Scheunert. A., M. Schieblich and J. Rescheke, 1935, A diet of mushrooms can thus supply vitamin and mineral nutrients in adequate amounts, *J.Z. Physiol, Chem.* **235**: 91.

Schisler, L.C. and J.W. Sinden, 1962, Nutrient supplementation of mushroom compost at spawning, *Mush. Sci.* **5**: 150–164.

Schisler, L.C., J.W. Sinden and E.H. Sigel, 1987, *Phytopathology* **57**: 519.

Sengbusch, R.V., 1968, The mushroom development, Maxplank Institute, Furkuturflan, Zensuchtung, *Mush. News* **16**(6): 4–14.

Seth, P.K., 1976, Supplementation of organic substrates of synthetic composts for increased mushroom yields, *Indian J. Mushrooms* **2**: 36–39.

Sethi, V. and J.C. Anand, 1978, Processing of mushrooms, *Indian Mush. Sci.* **1**: 233–238.

Shieh. N., 1981, A compost fermenting method by means of forced air circulation, *Mush. Sci.* **11**: 279–292.

Sinden, J.W., 1946, Synthetic composts for mushroom growing, *Bull. Pa. Agric. Exp. Stn.* **482**: 1–26.

Sinden, J.W. and E. Hauser, 1950, Report on two new mushroom dieseases, *Mush. Sci.* **1**: 96–100.

Sinden, J.W. and Hauser, E., 1950. The short method of compositing, *Mush. Sci.* **1**: 52–59.

Sinden, J.W. and E. Hauser, 1953, The nature of the composting process and its relation to short composting, *Mush. Sci.* **2**: 123–130.

Sinden, J.W. and L.C., Schisler, 1962, Nutrient supplementation of mushroom compost at casing, *Mush. Sci.* **5**: 267–280.

Singer, Rolf, 1961, Mushrooms and Truffles, Leonard Hill Books Ltd., pp. 272.

Song, C.H.,1986 Management of growing *Shiitake* in saw dust filled plastic bags. *Youth Commission,* Taiwan (in Chinese).

Soest Van, G.J.A., 1977, Possibilities of ventilation and cooking in the mushroom growing. *The Mushroom J.* **77**: 189–191.

Steineck, H., 1970, Gartenbaul Vers. Berichte **1970**: 104.

Stoller, B.B., 1943, Preparation of the synthetic composts for mushroom culture, *Pl. Physiology* **18**: 397–414.

Stoller, B.B., 1945, Experiments in mushroom culture, Ph.D. thesis, University of Wisconsin, Madison.

Stoller, B.B., 1952, Studies on the function of casing, part II, Some chemical and physiological characteristics of the casing soil and their effect on fruitification, M.G.A. *Bull* **36**: 352–360.

Stoller, B.B., 1962, Some practical aspects of making mushroom spawn, *Mush Sci.* **5**: 170–184.

Stoller, B.B., and J.F. Stauffer, 1968. The role of gamma radiation in mushroom growing, *Mushroom News* **16**(8): 13–20.

Straatsma, G. and R.A. Sampson 1993: Taxanomy of *Scytaldium thermophilum,* an important thermophilic fungus in mushroom compost. *Mycology Research* **97**: 321–328.

Straatsma, G., T.W. Olijnsma, J.P.G. Gerrits, J.G.M. Amsing, H.J.M. *Op. den Camp,* and L.J.L.D. van Griensven. 1994. Inoculation of *Scytaldium thermophilum* in mushroom compost and its effect on yield. *Applied and Environmental Microbiology* **60**: 3049–3054.

Su, U.T. and L.N. Seth, 1940. Cultivation of the straw mushroom, *Indian Farming* **1**: 332–333.

Tewari, R.P. and H.S. Sohi, 1978, Studies on the effect of depth of casing soil on mushroom production in *Agaricus bitortquis* (Quel) Sacc., *Indian Mush.* **1**: 263–266.

Tewari, R.P. and H.S. Sohi 1979, Cultivation of *Pleurotus sajor caju* (Fr.) Singer, *National Survival in Research, Production. Processing and Marketing of Mushrooms, Organised by* I.C.A.R.

Thomas, K.H., T.S. Ramakrishnan and I.L. Narasimhan, 1943. Paddy straw mushroom, *Madras Agr. J.* **31**: 57–59.

Tschierpe, H.J., 1973. Environmental Factors and mushroom growing, *Mush. J.,* (February): 77–94.

Vestiens, T. 1994. Tunnel composting technology. In: *Agaricus Compost.* N.G. Tan (ed) *Australian Mushroom Growers Association, Windsor, NSW, Australia* pp. 46–57.

Waksman, S.A. and C.A. Reneger, 1934. Artificial manure for mushroom production, *Mycologia* **26**: 38–45.

Wasson, G.R., 1969, Soma-Divine mushroom of immortality XIII, Heu Court Brace and World Inc., New York, p. 318.

Watt, B.K. and A.L. Merrill, 1963. Composition of foods, U.S. Dept. Agric. Handbook, 8.

Williams, B. and W.B. Esselen, 1946, *Mass. Agric. Exp. Station, Bull. No.* 434.

Wooster, H.A. Jr., 1954, Nutritional data, 2nd ed., H.J. Heirriz Co., Pitsburg, Pa.

Yin Guiling and N. Funner, 1988. Cultivation of Jew's ear on cotton seed hulls. *Mush. J. Tropics* **8**: 137–143.

Zaayen, Dideman-Van, 1972. Agricultural Research Report, 782, 130 pp.

Zeitlmayr, Linus, 1968, *Wild Mushrooms,* Frederick Muller, 138.

Index

D

E

F

G